A History of the
York – Scarborough Railway

by

Bill Fawcett

Hutton Press
1995

Published by

The Hutton Press Ltd.,
130 Canada Drive, Cherry Burton,
Beverley, East Yorkshire HU17 7SB

Copyright © 1995

Printed by
Image Colourprint Ltd.,
Grange Park Lane,
Willerby, Hull
HU10 6EB

ISBN 1 872167 71 3

The vast archive of documents, photographs and artefacts built up by Ken Hoole is now available for all students of transport and social history to consult. It is housed in the Ken Hoole Study Centre at Darlington Railway Centre and Museum, located in North Road Station. The collection is now owned by Durham County Council, while the Study Centre is operated by Darlington Borough Council, a commendable joint initiative by these two local authorities to safeguard the future of this unique treasury of railway history.

Contents

Gresley D49 Number 62750 heading out of Scarborough across Valley Road bridge, the former Washbeck Viaduct, on 2 April 1956. The carriage glimpsed on the left is standing in platform 2 of Londesborough Road Excursion Station. Photo: Ken Hoole.

Introduction

Scarborough, Queen of the Yorkshire Coast, has been a resort for three centuries but its fortunes were transformed 150 years ago, on 7 July 1845, when the railway was opened from York. The first mass excursion arrived a month later and the town soon became one of the most popular of British resorts, yet without sacrificing the relaxed charm of areas like the South Bay.

For its first 120 years the railway operated flat out at holiday time. Scarborough station grew, facilities expanded and it took all the skills of the railway staff to maintain smooth operation at peak periods. The last thirty years have seen the end of the traditional holiday business but the line now has a faster and more frequent regular train service than ever before and should have a useful role in future.

While I have long been fascinated by Scarborough, the idea for this history originated with the late Ken Hoole, the respected and authoritative historian of the railways of the north-east who lived near the town for many years. Just before his untimely death in 1988, he had begun a history of the line and I have been fortunate to be able to make use of his draft and research material in writing this account. Whilst my book is quite different from the one he would have published, I hope it would have met with his approval. Ken's extensive collection of railway documents, historical notes and photographs can be consulted in the study centre that bears his name at Darlington's North Road Station Museum. This provides a rich source of information for anyone interested in the railways of north-east England.

The principal archival source for this work is naturally the Public Records Office, at Kew, which holds the records of the railways concerned and their regulating department, the Board of Trade. York City Archives also have much relevant material, principally deposited plans and the records of the Ouse Navigation, and I am very grateful to the City Archivist, Mrs. Rita Freedman, for her assistance in exploring these. The libraries at York, Malton, and Scarborough have also been very helpful in tracing material; their local newspaper holdings are particularly useful. Over the years, British Rail has kindly provided access to architects' drawings which explain some of the mysteries of evolution of complex stations, such as Scarborough.

Many individuals have helped not just with factual material but in developing my understanding of the role and operation of the line; any misunderstandings that remain rest on my shoulders. I am grateful to Ken Appleby, Jack Layton, Scarborough's last stationmaster, Richard Pulleyn, George Sharp and Jim Shipley for sorting out some of these issues. I have also received valuable assistance from C.J. Emerson, Patrick Howat, J.R. Lidster, J.P. McCrickard, Hugh Murray, J.F. Sedgwick and K.L. Taylor.

Three people deserve special thanks. John Mallon, Scarborough's last goods agent, has made available a wealth of documentary and photographic material. John Addyman has prepared a number of drawings specially for this book and made a variety of constructive criticisms during its gestation. Colin Foster originally encouraged me to write it and has assisted greatly in the preparation for publication.

Inevitably, in confining 150 years history to one slim volume there will be ommissions. An obvious one is any account of the individuals who made the railway a success, particularly the operating staff at Scarborough. Their role is explored by Robin Lidster in his new book on Scarborough Station which should complement this one.

In conclusion, I should like to dedicate this book to the memory of Ken Hoole - *friend and mentor.*

Bill Fawcett
York, April 1995

MAP OF RAILWAY

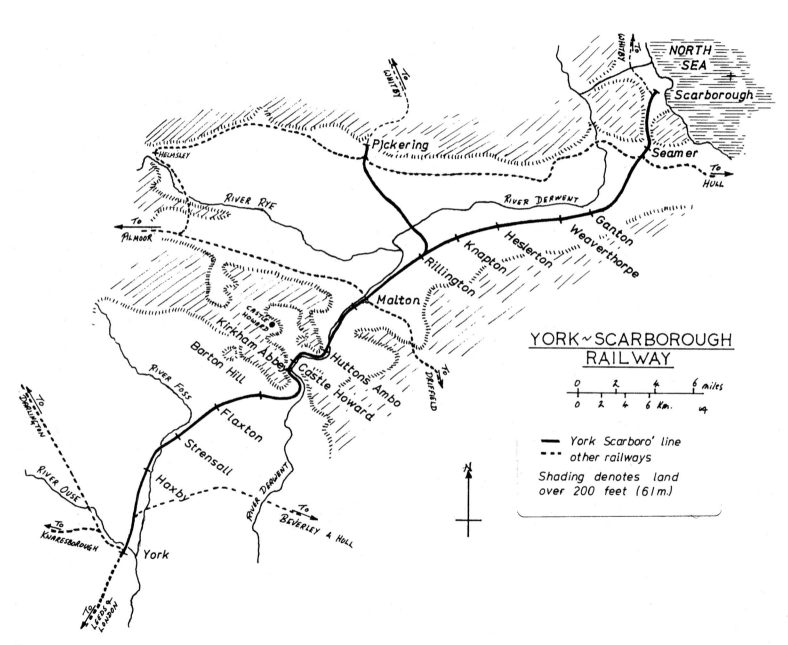

Chapter 1

Background and Promotion

Scarborough is best known today as a major tourist and conference centre - a role whose roots can be traced back to 1845, when the opening of the railway ushered in the era of *Monster Excursions* and masses of day visitors. Prior to this the town had been an exclusive resort for the Yorkshire gentry, and the flavour of these two aspects can still be savoured in the contrast between the quiet streets of large houses above the South Cliff and the bustling area close to the harbour.

Unlike Regency upstarts, such as Brighton, Scarborough was a town of some significance well before the fashion for *watering places* became established. The harbour, once the major harbour of refuge between the Humber and Tyne, nestles at the side of a promontory crowned by the gaunt ruins of the castle begun by King Stephen and these two formed the foci of a medieval walled town whose last gateway, Newborough, was unfortunately demolished in the early nineteenth century.

The founding of a spa, during the late seventeenth century, led to a new era in which the town began to spread genteel fingers across the hillside above the harbour. By 1831, Thomas Allen was writing in his *History of the County of York* that the *principal streets in the upper town are spacious and well paved, with excellent flagged footways on either side, and the houses have, in general, a handsome appearance. The new buildings on the cliff stand almost unrivalled in respect of situation, having in front a beautiful terrace, elevated nearly a hundred feet above the level of the sands.* The flavour of this Regency phase in Scarborough's growth can still be gleaned from the bow-fronted houses of York Place and the grander villas erected below the Crescent, such as Woodend which later provided the Sitwell family with a summer retreat from the increasingly industrialised surroundings of their family seat at Renishaw, near Sheffield.

Unlike Whitby, Scarborough has always been well situated for inland as well as marine communications. Behind the cliffs of the Yorkshire Coast rise two hill masses, culminating in the Wolds and the North York Moors, but these are separated by the broad, flat Vale of Pickering, through which winds the River Derwent, which rises in the hills to the north-west of the town and passes only four miles away before swinging west on its long journey to the Ouse. A glacial spillway, the Weaponess Valley, provides direct access from the town through the rump of these hills to the Vale at Seamer. Thus there is a good natural route inland from Scarborough, via the market town of Malton, to York and this is followed by both the main road (A64) and railway. In addition, since the Vale broadens out so much, a second route (A170) exists along its north side, following the foot of the North York Moors, to Pickering and Helmsley.

Before the coming of the railway, the chief communications along this corridor were the York-Scarborough road, turnpiked in 1752, and the Derwent Navigation. The latter originated with an Act of Parliament passed in 1702, which gave powers to make the river navigable up to Scarborough Mills although this was accomplished only as far as Malton. In 1720 the navigation was acquired by Thomas Wentworth, and his descendant, the second Earl Fitzwilliam, had an additional cut made in 1808 to extend it as far as Yedingham Bridge on the York-Scarborough turnpike. Made to a shallower depth than the earlier section, this could handle vessels up to 15 tons compared with 50 ton barges downstream of Malton. The principal traffic was coal coming into Malton, most of it originating at Earl Fitzwilliam's pits in the Barnsley area and travelling via the Aire & Calder Navigation and the River Ouse. In 1840 incoming coal totalled 37,898 tons; by comparison the tonnages exported from Malton, principally cereal crops, were quite small.[1]

The Derwent Navigation addressed the freight needs of Scarborough's hinterland but, ironically, made Hull the natural port to serve that area. It had little relevance to passenger transport, which was catered for by the York-Scarborough and Malton-Pickering turnpike trusts. The York-Scarborough turnpike followed a route generally similar to that of the present A64 but with some differences, notably at Knapton, six miles east of Malton, where the main road used to be the present B1258, crossing the Derwent at Yedingham and continuing through Snainton and Ayton as the present A170. The same trust operated the first stage of the road from Scarborough to Beverley, through Seamer.[2]

By 1840 a daily mail coach ran throughout the year from York to Scarborough, supplemented by a number of Summer-only services, including the *Old True Blue* from Leeds and the *Transit*

YORK & NORTH MIDLAND RAILWAY AND CONNECTING LINES IN 1841

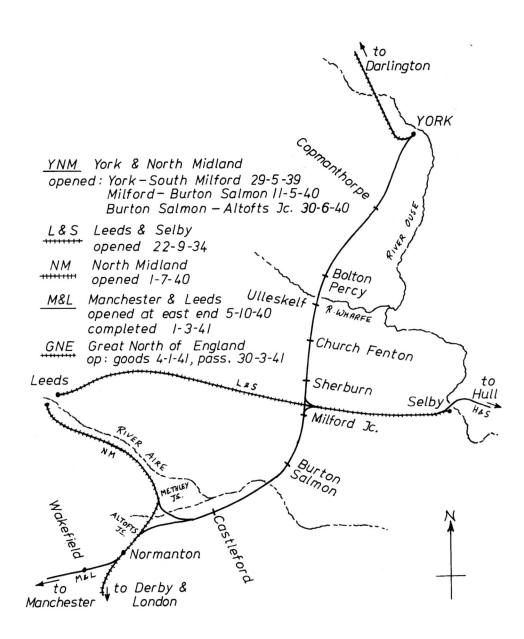

YNM York & North Midland
opened: York – South Milford 29-5-39
        Milford – Burton Salmon 11-5-40
        Burton Salmon – Altofts Jc. 30-6-40

L & S Leeds & Selby
       opened 22-9-34

NM North Midland
    opened 1-7-40

M&L Manchester & Leeds
     opened at east end 5-10-40
     completed 1-3-41

GNE Great North of England
     op: goods 4-1-41, pass. 30-3-41

to Darlington

YORK

Copmanthorpe

RIVER OUSE

Bolton Percy

Ulleskelf

R. WHARFE

Church Fenton

Sherburn

Selby

to Hull

H & S

Leeds

L & S

Milford Jc.

Burton Salmon

RIVER AIRE

NM

METHLEY JC.

ALTOFTS JC.

Castleford

Wakefield

Normanton

M & L

to Manchester

to Derby & London

N

from Sheffield.[3] Fares, however, were very high in relation to the earning power of the vast majority of people: twelve shillings inside (60p - equivalent to about two days' wages for a skilled artisan such as a railway engine driver) and nine shillings outside (45p) for the single journey from York to Scarborough, half this for the journey from Malton to either town. Passenger numbers were correspondingly low. During the four weeks commencing 16 July 1843 the Scarborough Mail carried only 168 passengers (60 inside and 108 outside) the full distance from York to Scarborough and 172 in the reverse direction, yet this was the height of the Summer Season; by comparison the four weeks beginning on 29 January 1843 brought only 61 outward passengers and 76 for the return trip.[4]

Any idea that travel, other than an occasional ride on the carrier's cart, was for ordinary people had to await the coming of the railway. In the event, the first of Yorkshire's coastal ports to obtain one was Whitby. This may appear strange nowadays, but Hull already had easy inland access via the Trent and Ouse while Scarborough had its gently graded turnpike road to Malton. Whitby was then a port of some significance, with fishing and whaling fleets and a sizeable shipbuilding industry, but poor inland communications because of the barrier posed by the North York Moors. To remedy this, a railway was built through the natural route to the Vale of Pickering, the glacial trough of Newtondale. Engineered by George Stephenson, it opened throughout on 26 May 1836. It was a modest affair, 24 miles long, worked by horses and hampered by a steep incline leading from the Lower Esk Valley up to the skirt of the moors at Goathland.

Whitby's railway terminated at Pickering, though it might have seemed advantageous to extend it as far as Malton and the Derwent Navigation. A coach service was established in connection with the railway, offering transport from York to Whitby at an inside seat fare of thirteen shillings (65p) or eight shillings (40p) outside; the railway's proportion of these fares was only four shillings (three shillings outside) although it accounted for nearly 50% of the total mileage, York-Pickering being about 26 miles.

At the same time another railway was being constructed from Leeds to Selby, to give the West Riding's rapidly-growing industrial capital better access to the River Ouse and to break the monopoly of the Aire and Calder Navigation. Carried out

by Telford's successor as President of the Institution of Civil Engineers, James Walker, it was a locomotive line, conceived on a much bolder scale than the Whitby & Pickering, and opened in 1834.

Any question of a railway to Scarborough clearly hinged on developments at York. There, a railway committee had been formed but was unable to decide between the rival attractions of a route to London, proposed by parties in Lincoln and Cambridge, and a direct line to Leeds - the latter being of more immediate benefit in bringing down the cost of coal to the city's manufacturers. This dilemma was resolved by events further south: the promotion of the Midland Counties and North Midland Railways to provide a route from Rugby, on the London & Birmingham Railway, to Leicester, Derby and Leeds.

The York & North Midland Railway Company (YNM) was formally set up at a meeting in York's Guildhall on 13 October 1835 and Stephenson was called in as engineer to report on a line to join the North Midland in the vicinity of Normanton. This was surveyed by his assistant, Frederick Swanwick, who had also surveyed the Whitby & Pickering, and with impressive speed the plans and Book of Reference were ready for deposit with the local Clerks of the Peace by the Parliamentary deadline of 30 November.

Despite problems with Lord Howden, at Grimston Park, the first YNM Bill received the Royal Assent on 21 June 1836, and the first section opened from a temporary station outside York's City Walls to a junction with the Leeds & Selby near South Milford on 29 May 1839. The final stage to Altofts Junction on the North Midland opened formally on 30 June 1840, with public services beginning the following day and providing a fastest time between York and London of ten hours.

Initially, the two chief activists in the YNM were James Meek and George Hudson. Meek, a Nonconformist and Radical, was a leading partner in the York Glassworks and keen to redress the competitive advantage of the manufacturing towns in the Yorkshire Coalfield. Hudson, later to be characterised by *Punch* as the *Railway King*, was a rising man of independent means, so far twice Lord Mayor of York and the unscrupulous leader of the dominant Tory group on the City Council. Born in 1800 in Howsham, a village on the River Derwent, he had become a draper in York but his situation was transformed in 1827 when he received a considerable inheritance from a great uncle. Thus, unlike industrialists such as Meek, he had time to spare for railway management.

Meek and Hudson were far from being natural allies, and in the Summer of 1839 Meek resigned from the YNM Board, of which Hudson was the Chairman. This was a protest against the running of Sunday trains, giving an interesting insight into the contemporary social conscience since Sunday was the only day of the week on which Meek's workpeople could escape their labours and avail themselves of the cheap excursion trains which the railways were already beginning to offer. Thereafter, Hudson achieved undisputed control of the railway and manipulated its accounts to achieve spectacular dividends (soon to reach an annual 10% but, unfortunately, largely paid out of capital). Thus he made his reputation as a railway promoter and built up a major empire over the next decade, before his exposure and ignominious downfall in 1849.

An extension of the YNM to Scarborough was a natural feature in Hudson's strategy. Indeed, as early as 19 October 1839 he and George Stephenson addressed a public meeting in Scarborough Town Hall on the subject of a railway, but it had to be deferred. By 1840 his immediate concern was the completion of a main line between York and Newcastle. In January 1841 the Great North of England Railway (GNE), largely promoted by the Quaker business community of Darlington, opened from York as far as Darlington but, having spent all its funds, the company was unable to proceed to the Tyne as originally planned.[5] Hudson took up the challenge and created the Newcastle & Darlington Junction Railway which was completed in 1844.

Not everyone welcomed the prospect of a railway to Scarborough. Apart from those with vested interests, such as Earl Fitzwilliam, there were people who felt, quite rightly, that it would undermine the town's exclusiveness as a resort. Ironically, the most vocal of these was a civil engineer, George Knowles, who had retired to Woodend and was a leading figure in the landscaping of the South Cliff. In 1840 he published a pamphlet claiming that the town *had no wish for a greater influx of vagrants and those who have no money to spend*, adding that *in a few years more the novelty of not having a railroad will be its greatest recommendation.*

Popular opinion was in favour of the railway, however, and Hudson was not the only promoter in the field. A survey was made by the engineer John Rennie (junior) for a line to York, and plans for this scheme, including a branch to Pickering, were deposited with the Clerk of the Peace for York on 29 February 1840 though not followed up by a Parliamentary Bill. Hudson took the precaution of having a survey made for the YNM, going over the route himself with George Stephenson during October, and as a holding operation both parties deposited rival plans in March 1841 and in 1842, so as to retain the option of promoting a Bill in the ensuing Parliamentary session.[6]

Both the Stephenson and Rennie schemes followed similar routes between Scarborough and Malton, keeping to the south side of the River Derwent. An alternative would have been to run along the north side, possibly continuing as far as Pickering so as to place this town on the main line rather than a branch - although this would have lengthened the route by up to five miles (8 kilometres).

West of Malton, the Derwent follows a winding valley, squeezed in between the Wolds and the Howardian Hills, before entering the Vale of York. Stephenson proposed to cross to the north bank at Low Hutton and then bypass the most tortuous bends by tunnelling for 1430 yards (1300m) under Whitwell Hill before reaching the turnpike at Spital Bridge (Barton Hill) and taking the present-day route past the villages of Flaxton and Strensall. Rennie's idea was to keep to the south bank and tunnel for 1100 yards (1000m) below the village of Westow before crossing the Derwent and heading to York by a more southerly route than Stephenson.

In 1843, with the Newcastle & Darlington Junction (NDJ) well advanced, the capital market looking healthy and his personal reputation standing high, Hudson decided to proceed with the Scarborough line. On 17 November YNM shareholders gave their consent, agreeing to the creation of an additional £260,000 capital to cover the cost, and at the end of the month plans were deposited for the third time with Hudson's friend and fellow YNM director Robert Davies, Clerk of the Peace and Town Clerk of York. On this occasion there was no rival scheme on the table.

This time the plans appeared in the name of Robert Stephenson, as engineer, although the survey was carried out under the direction of one of his assistants, John Cass Birkinshaw, who eventually supervised the line's construction. Now that Hudson was serious about the idea, significant changes had been made to the 1841 scheme - with a view to saving money and expediting construction. Originally, all turnpike roads and most township roads were to be crossed by bridges, now all but three had been replaced by level crossings.[7] Most important was the adoption of a sinuous route through the Derwent Valley instead of the tunnel, saving an estimated £30,000 and considerably speeding up construction.

The only really contentious change was in the route through York. To follow a direct line to Scarborough, the railway had first to cross the GNE, then the River Ouse before passing either by or through the village of Clifton. The GNE and YNM shared a joint station, a handsome Italianate terminus designed by Hudson's friend George Townsend Andrews, and in the 1841 scheme trains from Scarborough would have crossed the GNE main line on the level before reversing on the YNM main line to get into it.

In 1843, in order to get direct access without reversing, the Scarborough route was swung out on a wide curve, crossing the Ouse much further away from the city and, as a result, carving right through the middle of Clifton. This caused an outcry since the village was rapidly developing as a fashionable suburb. Local residents were not consoled by Hudson's offer of a station, and found a powerful advocate in Earl De Grey, formerly the principal landowner.

The protesters put forward several alternatives. One scheme to move the river crossing to the site of the present road bridge, Clifton Bridge, and pass through the Village Green was condemned by the City Council (Hudson's pliant tool) in their capacity as Trustees of the Ouse Navigation.[8] Another which,

more realistically, envisaged the line branching off the GNE just north of its Ouse Bridge near Skelton, was rejected by Parliament as placing the YNM too much in the hands of the GNE.

The Commons passed the York-Scarborough Railway Bill, with a third reading on 29 March 1844, but in the House of Lords De Grey's opposition proved decisive. After debating it during May, their Lordships also passed the Bill but only after inserting a clause which made the construction of the railway conditional on the written consent of the Clifton landowners (and occupiers). Thus neutered, the Act received the Royal Assent on 4 July 1844.

Even George Hudson, so used to getting his own way, had to admit defeat. On 5 August he returned to the City Council to secure their consent for a reversion to the 1841 route, with the line passing below the main street to the north, Bootham, and alongside the grounds of Bootham Hospital. The councillors cordially gave their approval, while expressing deep regret at the need for this change of route which was endorsed by Parliament in a further Act. This received the Royal Assent on 30 June 1845, barely in time for the opening of the railway on 7 July.

By now the GNE had passed into Hudson's hands, under the terms of a lease proposed in May 1845, and he therefore had less reason to regret Parliament's obliging him to make the Scarborough Branch commence at a junction with the GNE route into York Station, rather than the YNM, so as to avoid a level crossing of the two lines. Further consolation was provided by the Whitby & Pickering promoters, whose venture had not prospered and who were persuaded to sell their line to the YNM at a bargain price.

RAILWAYS OF YORK IN 1845

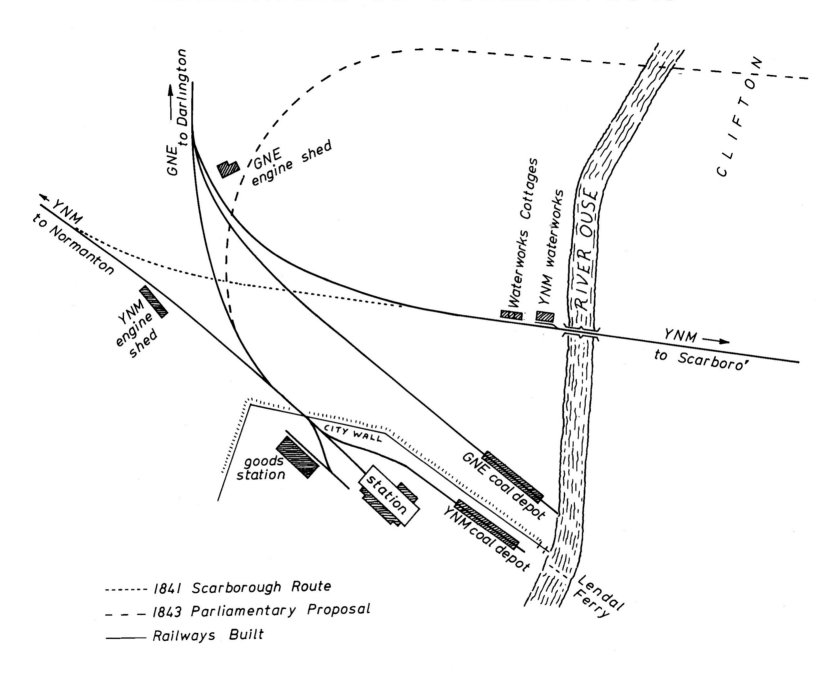

CLIFTON

GNE to Darlington

GNE engine shed

YNM to Normanton

YNM engine shed

Waterworks Cottages

YNM waterworks

RIVER OUSE

YNM to Scarboro'

CITY WALL

goods station

station

GNE coal depot

YNM coal depot

Lendal Ferry

------- 1841 Scarborough Route
- - - 1843 Parliamentary Proposal
——— Railways Built

Chapter 2

Building the Line

Apart from the Clifton conflict, Hudson's first Scarborough Railway Bill had enjoyed a relatively easy passage through Parliament. The only other major opponent was the third Earl Fitwilliam, the dominant landowner in the Malton area. His opposition was based on the loss of the Derwent Navigation's virtual monopoly of the town's trade, particularly in coal, and once Parliament had sanctioned this he came to terms with the progress of the railway.

Before construction could begin, the crucial step was to obtain the property required. Fortunately, substantial sections of the route lay in the hands of a few large landowners. By the Derwent, west of Low Hutton, it traversed the Earl of Carlisle's Castle Howard estate, though at Malton Earl Fitzwilliam's properties were interspersed with much smaller holdings.[1] Knapton was largely in the hands of James Tindall, followed by the Honourable Marmaduke Langley at West Heslerton and Sherburn, interrupted by Sir Tatton Sykes, of Sledmere, at East Heslerton. Sir Thomas Digby Legard held most of Ganton and Binnington, while for properties at Staxton and Seamer the company had to negotiate with William Joseph Denison. Proceeding from Seamer into Scarborough, the Mayor and Aldermen were responsible for significant portions of the route.

Hudson was in a hurry. He had promised shareholders that the line would open in July 1845, while his actual target was 17 June, the thirtieth anniversary of Waterloo, so the construction contracts were advertised to let before the first Act had even received the Royal Assent.[2] On 3 July 1844, the YNM Board considered the tenders received for the four sections into which the task had been divided, and decided to award all four contracts to Joseph Crawshaw, of Dewsbury in the West Riding. In return he accepted a 5% discount, bringing his total contract price down from £65,118 to £61,862.

Crawshaw was no stranger to the company. In 1837 he had become the contractor for the very first section of the YNM to be built, the 3.5 miles from York to Copmanthorpe, and followed this up with other work for them. The Scarborough line posed

him no serious problems, the only engineering works of any significance being the Ouse Bridge at York and those associated with the River Derwent at Low Hutton and Malton. Indeed, the nature of the route is best summed up in the remarkable statistic of only 25 bridges in 42 route miles.

Construction still had to wait on the company getting possession of the land but negotiations must have been brisk. Given Hudson's haste one might expect him to have ended up paying over the odds but the total land cost, at £111,633 including the Pickering Branch, was only £2,302 per mile. This compared with £2,414 on the original YNM and was well below the £3,854 per mile paid by the Great North of England Railway for comparable property.[3]

Most landowners were clearly cooperative and by the end of July 1844 work was underway near Scarborough, while on 19 October the Railway Times reported that the whole of the section from Malton to Scarborough had now been staked out. The major potential for delay lay in the Ouse Bridge, where the new route had to be agreed with the Clifton landowners, notably the Earl of Harewood who owned much of the property required between the river and Bootham. To speed construction Robert Stephenson adopted a two-span cast-iron girder bridge rather than the masonry arch structure which might have been expected.

The main construction base was located at Malton, halfway along the route and readily accessible via the Derwent Navigation. Memel Fir, required for the many timber bridges, was imported from the Baltic to Hull and only had to be transhipped once onto barges for the journey to Malton. Workshops were established there and George Kilburn, a joiner with previous experience of railway building, was employed by Crawshaw to supervise all the timber construction.[4] Though Robert Stephenson was the consulting engineer, he had many more important demands on his time and detailed design was handled by his assistant, John Cass Birkinshaw, based in York. Local supervision was provided by the resident engineer at Malton, Alfred Lamerte Dickens, twenty-two years old and the younger brother of the famous novelist.

Even after Crawshaw had won the contract, significant design changes continued to be made. Some bridges, such as the Norton Viaduct across the wetlands bordering the River Derwent east of

The YNM Road Bridge over the Derwent at Malton, looking west. The wagon on the right is on the siding serving the Derwent Mill.
Photograph : J. F. Mallon collection.

Malton, were intended from the outset to be built from timber; others were switched to timber in an attempt to save time and money. Thus the Derwent Bridge at Low Hutton was designed as a cast-iron structure, on similar lines to the Ouse Bridge at York, but some time in August 1844 Hudson agreed with his engineers that it should be built of timber instead. Such changes could cause confusion. At the Derwent Bridge, Kilburn found himself obliged to set up the temporary piles to support the *pile engines*, the gravity-operated piledrivers for the permanent bridge structure, before any plans became available. He worked instead to a centre line set out by Dickens some time in September until the drawings arrived from Birkinshaw two or three weeks later.

Railway builders were accustomed to problems, whether natural or man-made, and generally coped. Good progress was made with the works on the central section of the line, the Norton Viaduct being completed in December 1844, but the east end, between Seamer and Scarborough, brought troubles which it is

hard now to appreciate. The Weaponess Valley today is a well-drained tract of land, with the Mere featuring as an ornamental lake enclosed by tree-lined banks. In the eighteen-forties it was a peat bog, with the Mere just a somewhat wetter part than the rest. The navvies worked up to their knees in water cutting a shallow ledge out of the nose of Musham Bank, east of Seamer, and further on forming the line as the western boundary of the Mere. Much peat had to be excavated while the ground was consolidated under the direction of Peter Sharrock, employed by Crawshaw to supervise this section, and the work proceeded through the winter. However, despite these difficulties, the critical factor affecting the completion date was the settling of the route at York and the land purchases there.

This took a long time to resolve, and the foundation stone of the Ouse Bridge was not laid until 28 March 1845 but work then proceeded very rapidly. Early in May the level of the river was lowered at Naburn Lock to permit the sinking of piles for the centre pier and this was completed on 5 June, after which the workmen began laying the lower courses of stone. At the same time, work must have been proceeding hurriedly on the low twelve-arch brick viaduct carrying the line across the adjoining flood plain of Marygate Ings.[5] The railway navvies were not welcomed by all citizens, for the Ouse Navigation Committee recorded that Crawshaw should be *desired to prevent as much as he can a very intolerable nuisance which several of the workmen are guilty of in passing along the public walk*, namely the promenade recently formed in front of York's Museum Gardens.

Except for a short stretch beyond Bootham Hospital, where a minor landowner was holding out for an exorbitant price, the rest of the line was complete by 12 June, when a trial run was made from Bootham Stray to Scarborough. Meanwhile, the cast-iron girders had been brought to the bridge site by river and the work was finished with remarkable speed in time for the whole line to be formally inspected by Major General Pasley, of the Board of Trade, on 4 July, just 14 weeks since the commencement of the bridge and only a few days after the company had gained possession of the missing ground at Bootham by virtue of their second Act.[6] Having passed slowly along the main line and Pickering Branch to inspect the works, he made the journey back to York at 20 mph and pronounced himself satisfied with the Scarborough line itself and with the assistance, and no doubt the hospitality, offered by Hudson and his engineer. Pasley noted the need for a temporary speed restriction over a stretch at each end of the line where the ballasting was still incomplete although 200 men were engaged on this. The Pickering Branch was less advanced, much ballasting remaining to be done, but he was happy to approve its opening for horse-drawn passenger trains, which suited the YNM since they wanted to delay locomotive working until a substantial part of the Whitby & Pickering had been reconstructed to take locomotives.

Hudson rarely missed the opportunity for a public show and the following Monday, 7 July, the Scarborough line was duly opened in style.[7] After breakfast at York Guildhall, the guests boarded a train of 35 carriages, drawn by the aptly-named locomotives *Hudson* and *Lion*. A local reporter referred to its *huge snake-like body* which, not surprisingly, had difficulties reversing at the junction with the GNE. At Castle Howard Station the train was met by Lord Morpeth and the party enjoyed the hospitality of his father, the Earl of Carlisle, who provided a *supply of strong ale* from his cellars. The train stopped again at the yet-incomplete

Malton Station and then proceeded on its way under a triumphal arch at Rillington, the junction for Pickering, having been joined by Birkenshaw and a party of directors who had earlier inaugurated the service on that branch. It was serenaded by a band at Sherburn and again at Ganton, where Sir Thomas Legard joined the party. Finally, it arrived at Scarborough at 1.35, having left York three hours earlier. The town was en fete, the shops were closed and the happy day declared a Public Holiday.

The train was met by the Mayor and a crowd of spectators estimated at between ten and fifteen thousand. The station being incomplete, luncheon was served under a temporary roof and the usual fulsome speeches were made, while the Mayor of Scarborough proposed the toast to *that King of Railway Directors - George Hudson*. After a brief procession through the town, the passengers re-embarked and got back to York shortly after 6 p.m. This left plenty of time to prepare for dinner at the Guildhall, with entertainment from Walker's brass band and a party of glee singers, together with more speeches - including one from George Stephenson.

For Hudson, the opening of the Scarborough line and the branch to Pickering provided a springboard for expansion across the North and East Ridings. The Whitby & Pickering was already in his net, while Parliament had authorised the YNM to construct a branch from Seamer, 3 miles from Scarborough, along the coast to Bridlington where it would link up with a line from Hull, promoted by the Hull & Selby Railway but actually built by Hudson after he took over that company as well. For the moment, however, the new line settled down to a daily passenger service of three trains each way, with one on Sundays, although this was almost immediately augmented with excursion traffic - the first day trip from Newcastle being advertised for 5 August.[8]

The formal opening of the line did not mean that construction was over, simply that it was usable. As well as the principal stations - at Scarborough the early trains arrived at a temporary wooden platform - work was still continuing on the formation itself, for Hudson, in a shortsighted piece of economy, had decreed that the line be built as a single track although land was purchased to accommodate two. He soon changed his mind and on 22 January 1845 the YNM Board decided to lay double track between York and Malton but this meant widening the earthworks and bridges, a task which had not been completed by the time of the opening. East of Malton, the widening began later

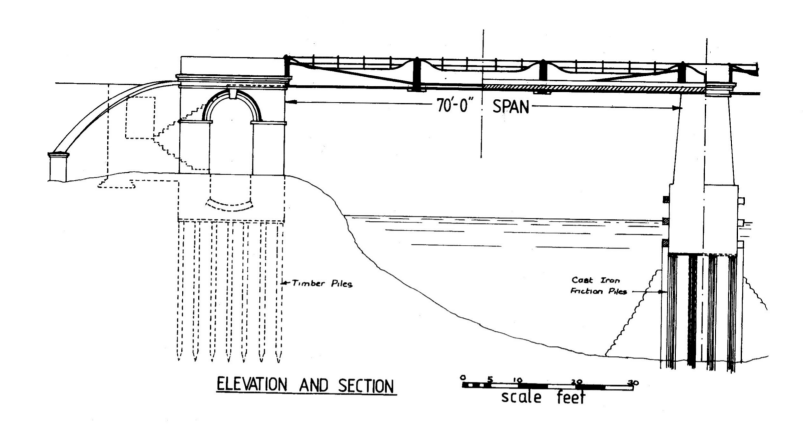

70'-0" SPAN

Timber Piles

Cast Iron
Friction Piles

ELEVATION AND SECTION

scale feet

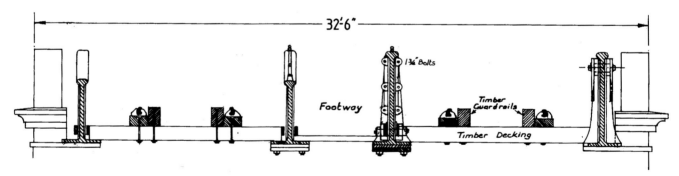

32'-6"

1¾" Bolts

Footway

Timber
Guardrails

Timber Decking

SECTIONS OF SUPERSTRUCTURE   2 X SCALE

Scarborough Railway Bridge, York.
Drawing by J. F. Addyman, based on the
original contract drawings.

and had to proceed while keeping the existing line operational; as a result the work was prolonged and at the beginning of February 1846 it was still expected to take a further six weeks.[9]

Turning to the railway itself, the engineering features, though few, are of significant interest. They are probably best considered by taking a journey along the line as it stood soon after the opening. Leaving the junction with the GNE, half a mile outside York Station, the railway proceeded through a shallow cutting spanned by a brick arch, carrying Thief Lane and one of only three overbridges. Next came Robert Stephenson's Ouse Bridge, a characteristic example of his trussed cast-iron girder designs, with the added novelty of employing cast-iron piles to speed construction. Unlike the many timber bridges, which have been totally reconstructed, much of this survives.

Stephenson's ingenuity was called upon because cast iron is a fickle material, very good in compression but prone to fracture unexpectedly when in tension or in shear stress. Wrought-iron, by contrast, is a ductile material which behaves elastically in tension and will only deform permanently if overstressed. Stephenson built each span of the bridge using four simple, straight cast-iron beams. Since these were too long to cast as single girders, each was formed from three lengths, bolted end-to-end through joining flanges. One pair carried the roadway for each track, while a pedestrian footpath was borne in the middle of the bridge between the lines. As was common practice, he made the bottom flange of each girder much larger than the top one, thereby reducing the stress in it and providing a large surface on which to rest the continuous wooden deck. The rails were borne on waybeams attached to this deck, and wooden guardrails were provided to check the train wheels in the event of a derailment.

When a train runs onto such a bridge, the girders begin to sag - the upper flange being compressed and the lower one going into tension - hence Stephenson's thickening of the bottom flanges. In addition he used wrought-iron tension bars, tied across the three component sections of each girder and pivotting on pins fixed into them. Though not evident from the surviving drawings, it is likely that he included some facility for tensioning these bars to pull the bottom flange of the girder into compression. Loading by a train would probably still draw these flanges into tension but to a much lower level of stress, due to their pre-compression and the sharing of stress with the tie bars.

So much for the theory. In practice these tie bars introduced local areas of high stress into the girders, notably at each end where they were anchored just above the point of maximum shear stress - where the girder sits on the edge of its masonry abutment. To combat this, Stephenson thickened the girders at these points so that they formed, in effect, miniature cast-iron columns to carry the load from the tension bars down onto the abutments. In addition, he carried the haunches of the girders well back from the edge of each abutment. A curious omission, if the original drawings are to be believed, is that there were no transverse ties to hold the girders in place.

Whether the trussed girder, in this form, was a satisfactory design is open to debate. It worked reliably in static structures, such as Portsmouth Dockyard's Number 6 Boathouse, also completed in 1845 and still standing, but was soon to be discarded for railway bridges in circumstances which nearly ended Robert Stephenson's career. As engineer to the Chester & Holyhead Railway he designed a similar bridge with 98 feet (29.9 m) spans across the River Dee at Chester. This opened for traffic in October 1846 but only lasted until the following May when one girder broke under a passing train; all but the locomotive fell into the river and five people were killed.[10] Strangely, the Dee Bridge seems to have been inferior in a number of details to that at York. The roadways were carried on a number of separate cross beams resting on the bottom flanges, thereby concentrating the stress at discrete points rather than distributing it along each girder. The tracks were ballasted with stone, adding considerably to the dead weight of the structure, and on the afternoon of the accident Stephenson had supervised the addition of a further layer of ballast to damp out vibrations - probably the last straw that broke the camel's back.

The Board of Trade reacted by asking all railway companies for details of their cast-iron bridges and the YNM took the lesson of the Dee Bridge to heart by strengthening the Ouse Bridge. Cast-iron shoes were fixed onto the land abutments and middle pier, and timber props were set into these, thereby converting the structure into a primitive arch - the only reliable type of cast-iron bridge.

Cast iron found an apparently novel use in the centre pier of the structure. The land abutments are built of sandstone and rest on wooden piles driven into the ground, in the absence of a bedrock near the surface. Normally, the middle pier would have been

The original railway bridge over the River Ouse at York, opened in 1845. This had a public footpath between the two tracks, reached by stairs inside each abutment. The bridge was renewed in 1875 using the original abutments and centre pier, and although the footpath was retained it was placed on the east side and the abutment stairways abandoned. Ken Hoole collection.

The same bridge, showing the wooden props added following the collapse of the similar Dee Bridge in May 1847. Ken Hoole Collection.

18

built in the same way, employing a cofferdam to keep the water away during construction. To save time, cast-iron friction piles were sunk into the river bed and left standing proud to within a few feet of the river's surface. The water level, which is held up artificially by a weir at Naburn, was lowered to facilitate piling and to permit the construction of the lower courses of masonry on top of these piles. Stone was tipped between and around the piles to protect them but the river tended to scour it out again and tipping was still going on as late as December 1845, when the Ouse Navigation Committee were compelled to point out that it was becoming a hazard to shipping.[11]

Despite doubts about its strength, Stephenson's *Scarborough Railway Bridge*, as it is commonly known, remained in use for almost thirty years, handling much heavier loads than the original YNM trains. It was eventually rebuilt in connection with the provision of a completely new station at York, which required the tracks to be at a higher level than they had been originally. To raise them by four feet (1.2m), the abutments were retained but the cast-iron beams were replaced by deep wrought-iron lattice girders while the footpath was moved from its rather alarming position between the tracks over to the east side of the bridge. The walled-up entrance to the original pedestrian steps can still be seen within the archway of the north abutment. The well-known ironfounder John Butler, of Leeds, won the contract for the rebuilding in December 1872, with a tender of £3,918, and the work was completed in July 1875.[12]

Scarborough Bridge still had a trick in store. Two years later, during a temporary lowering of the river, the North Eastern Railway's engineers observed that the south abutment was beginning to subside. For a year they monitored the situation, which was caused by the river scouring the rock originally dumped under the southern span and eroding the south bank; the direction of the current meant there was no comparable problem on the opposite bank. The NER then approached the Ouse Navigation Committee for permission to dump more rock below the bridge but this was refused, York's City Engineer, George Styan, pointing out that this could only make matters worse in the long term by increasing the scouring of the bank itself.[13] The railway were told to pile the bank instead, and in the course of stabilising the abutment they walled up the original arch over the riverside path.

Once across the river, the Scarborough line passed over a short embankment followed by the low brick viaduct across the flood plain. Raising the tracks here in the eighteen-seventies entailed tipping earth over these arches which are entirely hidden in the resulting embankment.

Even in low-lying York, the land eventually rises from the river and so the railway entered a cutting before passing under Bootham by the second of the original overbridges. Handsome cast-iron railings crown the walls of the cutting, while the bridge deck extends beyond the roadway and was intended to carry an overtrack station building with stone steps leading down to the platforms below. This was never built, although the people of Bootham and Monk Wards petitioned Hudson for a station in 1846 and the great man replied that he felt the importance of providing one. Instead, the YNM Board in June 1848 authorised the construction of a booking office serving a temporary station near Bootham Stray, which was a venue for agricultural shows and similar events.[14]

The first permanent station was reached at Haxby, four miles from York, and before the next, Strensall, the line crossed the canalised River Foss. There were no further engineering features of any significance until Low Hutton where, after twisting for several miles along the north bank of the Derwent, the line finally crossed the river. This was achieved by a wooden viaduct with four main spans of 50 feet (15.2m) set at a 28 degree skew. This was begun in September 1844 as a three-span bridge with brick abutments but progress was delayed because the contractors could not gain access to the west bank until the beginning of the following year. Possibly work was skimped in the rush to get it finished, at any rate just as the timber decking was being assembled the west abutment fell. Birkinshaw then abandoned the attempt to found an abutment close to the riverbank and introduced the fourth span.[15]

Further on, before reaching Malton, the line crossed a loop in the river by means of two low timber bridges, but by then it had come down to barely ten feet (3.3m) above the normal water level so a straight cut was made across the neck of the loop to preserve the navigation. A year after the opening of the railway there were still complaints that the new cut was not deep enough for shipping and the YNM determined to have it deepened at the expense of Crawshaw, the contractor.[16]

The Derwent Bridge at Low Hutton, looking east. Photo : Bill Fawcett.

Valley Road Bridge today. In the centre is the 1881 skew arch; to its left can be seen a blocked up arch of the original Washbeck Viaduct. Photo: Bill Fawcett.

While the bridges across the old loop were eventually superseded by embankments and a culvert, that at Huttons Ambo was replaced in 1867 by a wrought-iron girder structure.[17] Earlier, there had been a passenger ferry at this point but this appears to have been superseded unofficially by pedestrians using the railway bridge instead. The YNM and NER were probably quite happy with this since it provided access to Huttons Ambo Station for people living on the south bank of the river, especially since the population of the station's catchment area was estimated to be only about 400. However, the proprietors on the south bank, Menethorpe Estates, complained of trespass and so in 1885 the NER constructed a light suspension footbridge over the Derwent, making effective use of old rails and with the estate contributing £50 towards its £300 cost.[18]

All trace of the original Derwent railway bridge has vanished and the present structure combines the yellow brick piers of the 1867 bridge with a later set of plate girders. There are four of these, directly bearing the waybeams of the rails, with footways cantilevered from the outer ones. The river piers are borne by iron piles which extend well above the normal water level, to avoid the need for cofferdams during their construction.

At Malton the YNM built a wooden roadbridge across the Derwent, leading via a new street, Railway Street, to Yorkersgate and the town centre. Though replaced in 1870 by a wrought-iron girder structure, it was photographed and provides some idea of the likely appearance of the other timber bridges.[19]

East of Malton Bridge, the Derwent used to sprawl across the site of the railway and so its south bank was partially straightened out and a long low timber viaduct provided across the wetlands adjoining the township of Norton. This again has vanished as the river has been tamed, being infilled during the early months of 1868, when the opportunity was apparently taken to raise the line so as to reduce the flood risk.[20] From here to Ganton the line kept to the southern fringe of the bottom of the Vale of Pickering, just where the land is beginning to slope up towards the foot of the Wolds, and then crossed the once-marshy levels of Seamer Carr to the head of the Weaponess Valley.

Proceeding down the valley, the railway made its way across the bogland at the Mere then climbed a little before swinging across the valley of the Wash Beck on a brick arch viaduct of five 25 feet (7.6m) spans. This appears to have been constructed without piling, the foundations of the piers being laid in holes cut deep into the clay. Work was delayed, possibly because of Hudson's resiting of the terminus north of Love Lane; it only began on 17 April 1845 and the rush to finish may have compromised the bridge's long-term stability. In 1881 the North Eastern Railway widened it to carry extra tracks and replaced the middle three arches by the present massive skew arch over Valley Road.[21] This was widened again in 1907 in connection with the building of Londesborough Road excursion station.

Finally came the third of the original overbridges, bridge number 25, carrying Love Lane (now Belgrave Terrace) over the approach to the Scarborough terminus. No doubt once similar to its counterpart in Bootham, this also was a late starter, only begun in June 1845 shortly before the line was about to open so that for several months the roadway was carried over a temporary wooden bridge. During construction the west abutment had to be rebuilt as Sharrock, supervising this section, had been given an erroneous drawing, possibly indicating a batter (a slope of the walls) which was not intended; Birkinshaw, the engineer, was not sympathetic - when he saw the work going wrong he told Sharrock that he should have known better - despite the drawing. This bridge was first rebuilt in 1865 to facilitate one of the many enlargements of the passenger station.[22]

The Pickering Branch was a very straightforward affair with no engineering features of note, traversing the flat bed of the onetime Lake Pickering and crossing the River Derwent at a point where it has shrunk to very modest proportions, upstream of its confluence with the River Rye. Marishes Bridge was a low timber viaduct, 500 feet (152m) long, spanning the river and the adjoining meadows. Over the years portions of this were gradually infilled, with the central section finally being replaced by a wrought-iron girder bridge completed in October 1868.[23]

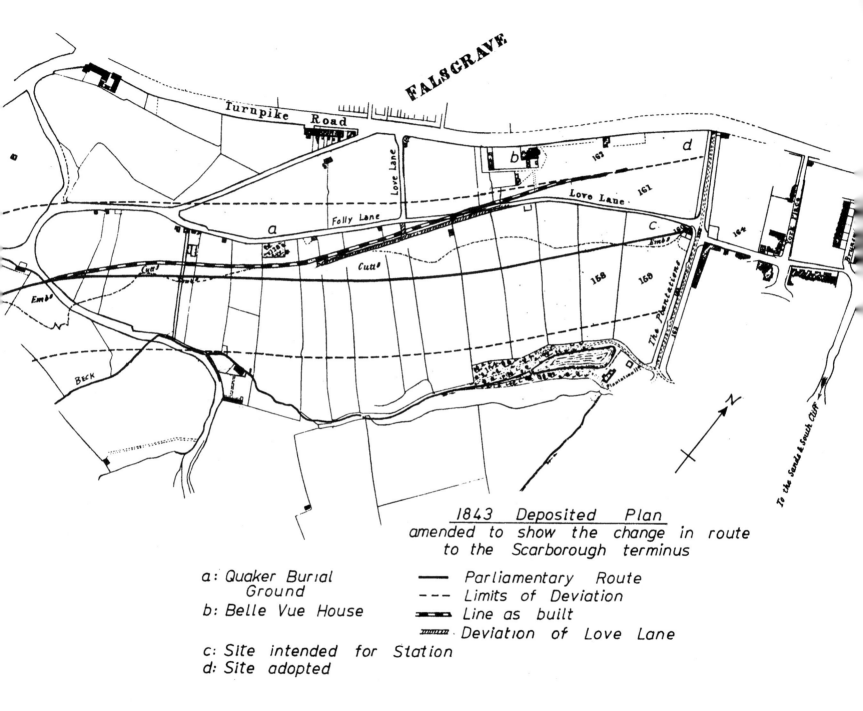

FALSGRAVE

Turnpike Road

Love Lane

Folly Lane

a

b

Love Lane 161

c

d

163

164

168

166

Cutt⁵

Cutt⁹

Emb⁵

Beck

The Plantations

Plantation Hill

162

N

To the Sands & South Cliff

1843 Deposited Plan
amended to show the change in route
to the Scarborough terminus

a: Quaker Burial Ground
b: Belle Vue House
c: Site intended for Station
d: Site adopted

——— Parliamentary Route
- - - Limits of Deviation
▬▬▬ Line as built
▭▭▭ Deviation of Love Lane

A portion of the 1843 Deposited Plan, modified to show the resiting of the Scarborough terminus north of Love Lane.

Chapter 3

Early Stations and Other Buildings

In common with other YNM enterprises, the design of the stations and other buildings on the Scarborough line was placed in the hands of Hudson's friend George Townsend Andrews. Though he was born in Exeter, Andrews became established in York around 1826, when he was only 22 years old, as the junior partner of a fashionable London architect and soon built up an extensive practice. This reached its peak during the eighteen-forties when, in addition to a large output of railway work, he was designing a number of major buildings in York including St. John's College, the De Grey Rooms and the former Yorkshire Insurance Company Head Office. Despite this he is best known for his railway stations, which are of an almost uniformly high standard and of which this line still provides some fine examples, not least the terminus at Scarborough itself.

In order to proceed with land purchases, the choice of station sites was an early priority. In August 1844 Hudson was to be found in Malton settling not only the site for the station, actually located in Norton on the opposite bank of the Derwent, but a route for a new river bridge and street leading up to Yorkersgate.[1] The Scarborough station took longer to sort out because the terminus was resited. The deposited plans show that it was originally intended to carry the line south of Love Lane (now Westwood), and land was purchased there for this purpose, but the station was instead built on more level ground to the north of the lane and with a frontage directly onto the main street, Westborough. Site constraints meant that the original coal depot and the locomotive shed were placed much further west, at either end of the Washbeck Viaduct, near the village of Falsgrave.

The contracts for the buildings were let in February 1845 and came to a total of £38,121.[2] At 63% of the value of Crawshaw's first civil engineering contract, this emphasises the importance which Hudson attached to the public image of the railway, as exemplified in its stations - particularly the Scarborough terminus.

This comprised a spacious trainshed, covering two platforms and tracks which could be used at night for carriage storage.[3] Following contemporary practice, turnplates and cross tracks gave access between these lines for shunting the very short-wheelbase locomotives and carriages of that period, but these were rapidly rendered useless by developments in engines and rolling stock. The design was derived from that of Andrews' earlier terminus at York and comprises a hipped roof in two spans, borne on three sides by stone walls and with a cast-iron arcade supporting the valley down the centre. The light wrought-iron roof trusses are based on those pioneered at Euston Station by Robert Stephenson and Charles Fox and employ L-shaped beams for those members subject to bending moments, the principals, purlins and struts, and round bars for the tie rods. With the loss of Euston and many other early stations, the Scarborough trainshed is now the finest example of this early period to survive in use in Great Britain, although there is a comparable work in Dublin: Sancton Wood's Kingsbridge Station (now Heuston) of 1846.

One important innovation, compared with York Station, was the treatment of the open end of the shed, where the tracks enter. At York, as at Andrews' Durham Gilesgate and Gateshead Greenesfield stations (both 1844), this was not open at all; instead each track entered through an individual doorway in a substantial masonry wall. At Scarborough this wall was replaced by an arcade similar to that down the middle of the shed and formed from cast-iron spandrel panels bolted onto slender octagonal columns.

Characteristically, in composing the station frontages Andrews gave most prominence to the trainshed, whose terminal end has an impressive facade with arched windows set between boldly rusticated pilasters. At right angles to this was the comparatively modest single-storey office range, facing onto a forecourt separated from Westborough by handsome cast-iron railings. A due sense of dignity was imparted by a portico of paired Tuscan columns from which two archways led into a spacious booking hall, with a semicircular office counter projecting from the rear wall. The already customary facilities, waiting rooms and toilets, were reached from the adjoining platform. At the southwest end was a suite of refreshment rooms culminating in an elegant dining room, whose expensive pier glasses proved a sore point with disgruntled shareholders sorting out the YNM's finances after Hudson's enforced departure in 1849.[4]

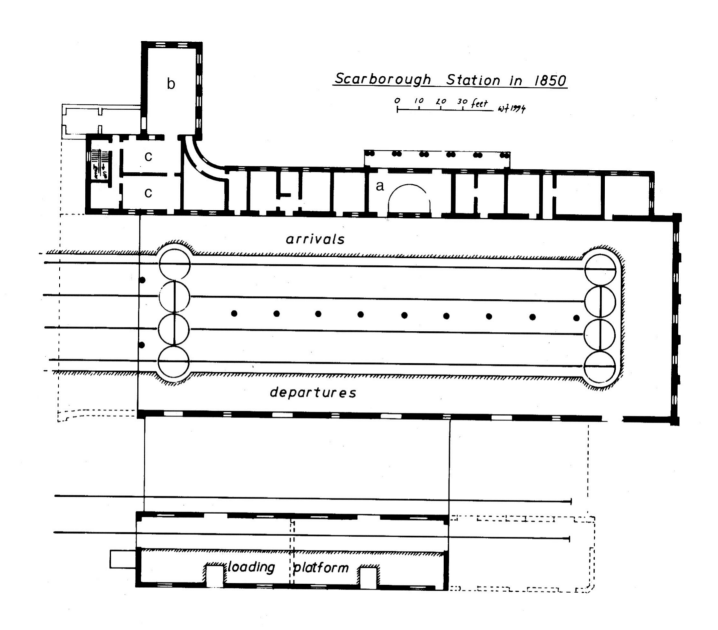

Scarborough Station in 1850

0 10 20 30 feet wf 1994

b

c

c

a

arrivals

departures

loading platform

Ground Plan of Scarborough Station in 1850: a is the booking hall b is the dining room c are the refreshment rooms. Bill Fawcett.

Scarborough Station with B16/3 (rebuilt NER Class S3) Number 61434 standing at platform 6 in the nineteen-fifties. To the left is the cast-iron arcade bearing the end of the main trainshed roof. On the right is the lenticular truss of the link span. Photo : Ken Hoole.

Malton Station, looking west about 1974. The up platform had been removed but Andrews' trainshed remained with William Bell's 1883 verandah roofing in the foreground. The wooden boarding seen above the "gentlemen" sign covered the original locomotive water tank. Photo: Bill Fawcett.

Scarborough Station in 1995 with a Class 158 Sprinter about to depart for York. Dismantling some roof cladding for repair has shed light on the arcade running down the centre of the trainshed. The stone bases of the columns were exposed when the tracks were lowered to obtain adequate platform heights. Photo: Bill Fawcett.

A surviving Andrews' drawing implies that Hudson contemplated providing a hotel, as he had done at his Gateshead terminus the previous year. Perhaps realising that this would be a needless provocation to Scarborough's hoteliers he did not proceed with the idea, although a few bedrooms were provided at some stage and during the late nineteenth century were advertised as a hotel: probably for commercial travellers rather than holidaymakers.[5]

The second station in importance was Malton, which also boasted a trainshed, albeit a single span of 40 feet (12.2m), with a central supporting column to each of the hipped ends of the roof.[6] As befits a country town, its facade was much less formal than that of Scarborough, being an asymmetrical composition of a single-storey office range and a two-storey villa for the stationmaster, both having hipped roofs with deep, coved eaves. Originally there were two tracks through the station with a platform either side, each bearing a small water tower to serve the locomotives, but all this was to alter quite soon as Malton developed into a junction.

The wayside stations were based on designs which Andrews had originally explored in his work for the Great North of England Railway and further developed on the Newcastle & Darlington Junction. Hudson's wholesale adoption of level crossings meant that Andrews was able to compose the larger stations as modest two-storey villas with a relatively formal, symmetrical facade towards the road and a more picturesque appearance seen from the railway. Stylistically they are an amalgam of late Georgian and Italianate concepts, the latter showing up particularly in the low-pitched roofs with their deep overhang. Most were executed in the common clamp brick, with fine orange gauged brick being used in an attractive contrast for the window and door lintels. Between Kirkham Abbey and Huttons Ambo use was made of limestone from the nearby Hildenley Quarries, which also supplied the masonry for Malton Station.

An early view of the railway at Malton. The passenger station is on the right and the 1857 goods station is seen in the centre. Valentine Rippon Collection.

A good example of Andrews' style is provided by the station at Haxby. The house is entered through a sandstone doorcase, based on the entrance to the Palazzo Farnese in Rome, one of the architect's favourite sources of inspiration. The stationmaster's office is, characteristically, provided with a bay window, giving a view up and down the platform. Adjoining it is a small waiting room, which, prior to the building of an additional bedroom above, would have had its roof extended to shelter a small portion of the platform. A similar design is met at Kirkham Abbey, though with an extra room intruding on the front of the building, and a variant at Knapton, where the doorcase is supplanted by a projecting porch. The most flamboyant development is at Castle Howard, where the tracks are overlooked by a boldly corbelled-out balcony in the style of a Palladian window. As well as the distinguished owner of the castle this also catered for important visitors, including on an early occasion Queen Victoria.

A curious and rather unsatisfactory variation on the Haxby theme occurs at Rillington. Although this station serves the village its role was conceived primarily as that of the junction for the Pickering line, so the station house was oriented towards the platform with its formal entrance set between a pair of bay windows, serving the office and waiting room. The platforms were sheltered by a trainshed, to which the house seemed a rather slight appendage.

Strensall station introduces the motif of a pair of arched windows in its gable, a feature which appears also in many of the gatekeepers' cottages and in two of the stations built as single-storey cottages. Like Kirby, on the Pickering Branch, these one-storey stations conform to an H plan, with gabled wings breaking forward either side of a stretch of platform (or rather paving) sheltered by an overhang of the main roof. Huttons Ambo and Heslerton had arched windows, the former also distinguished by a self-consciously picturesque chamfering of the corners of its roof, while Flaxton and Kirby had bay windows.

The growing demands of stationmasters' families led the North Eastern Railway (NER) to extend many of the station houses and the effects of this are naturally most obvious at those which had just one storey. In 1870 Heslerton gained an upper floor, though symmetry was maintained; Flaxton was less carefully handled, having extra bedrooms piled on top of one end in 1881, but Huttons Ambo retains its original appearance, having been extended by building another block on behind.[7]

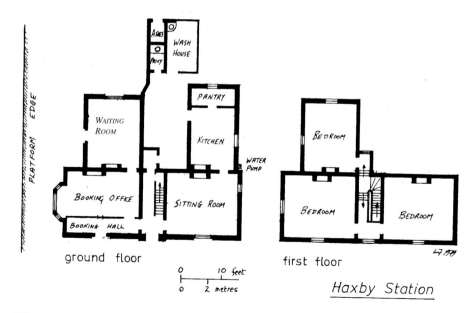

ground floor   first floor

Haxby Station

Haxby Station - ground plan as built.
Bill Fawcett.

28

Haxby Station - elevations, including extra bedroom added above waiting room. Bill Fawcett.

Seamer goods shed during demolition in 1978
Photo: Bill Fawcett.

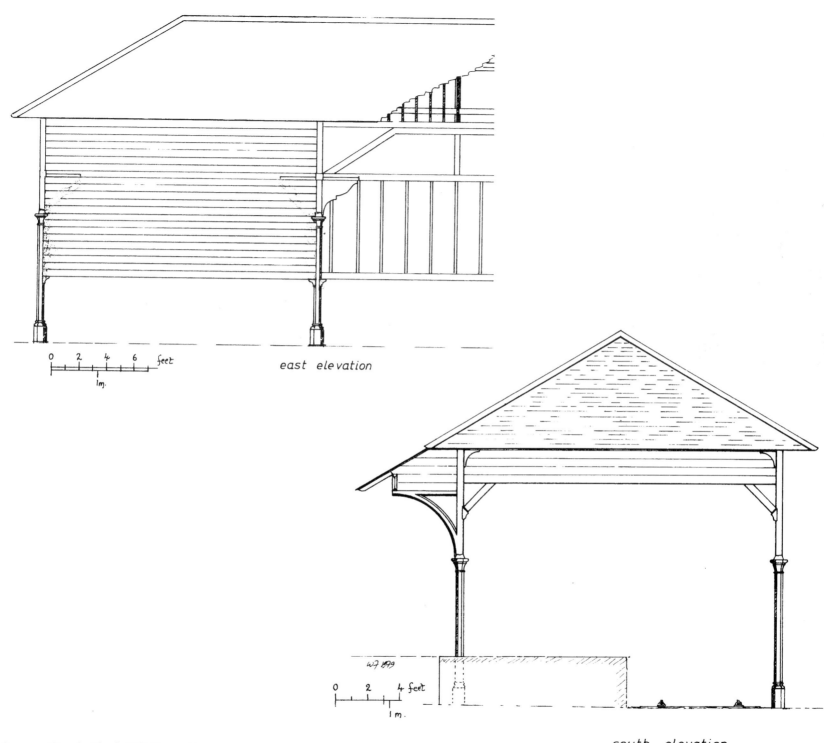

east elevation

0 2 4 6 feet

1m.

W7 1979

0 2 4 feet

1m.

south elevation

Seamer Goods Shed. Bill Fawcett.

31

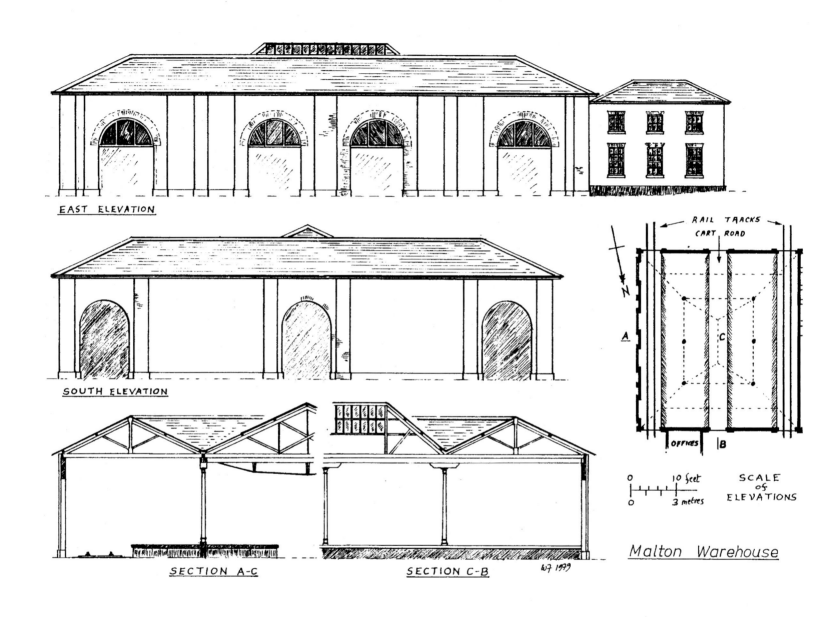

EAST ELEVATION

SOUTH ELEVATION

SECTION A-C

SECTION C-B

WF 1979

RAIL TRACKS

CART ROAD

N

A

C

OFFICES

B

0   10 feet

0   3 metres

SCALE
of
ELEVATIONS

Malton Warehouse

The NER Goods Station at Malton, built in 1856-7. Drawing: Bill Fawcett.

Malton and Scarborough had substantial platforms, formed with huge sandstone flags (probably Elland landings), although these were originally much lower than at present. Provision at other stations was less generous, basically just a flagged area in front of the building, and the addition of platforms to Board of Trade standards led to some curious anomalies, as at Strensall where the station building was left on the opposite side of the level crossing from the later platform. Seamer underwent more radical changes. With the opening of the branch to Filey on 5 October 1846 and the completion of the coastal route to Hull a year later, it became a significant junction and was eventually provided with an island platform, quite divorced from the station house.

Many of the stations were equipped also with goods sheds. Only at Malton and Scarborough were these masonry structures, otherwise they were constructed from timber and cast-iron, which made for speed of erection. Some stations, such as Huttons Ambo, had no goods shed at all. Andrews' design for these is typified by the shed at Seamer, which was the last to survive, being demolished in 1978. A hipped roof was supported on two lines of octagonal cast-iron columns. It covered a single railway track and the adjoining transhipment platform, while brackets on the roadside columns carried an extension of the roof to provide some shelter for carts loading there.

Scarborough goods shed lay just behind the passenger station and was a brick building housing a single track and a platform. The wall facing the station was given an attractive arcaded treatment, while a single doorway in the one opposite led into a cart bay in the platform. The roof was continued at one end on cast-iron columns to form an open-sided loading area, an arrangement which can still be seen at Driffield, despite infilling. Between 1846 and 1849 the goods shed was doubled in length and linked to the passenger station by a single span roof.

The resulting ensemble demonstrates rapid developments in roof design. The goods shed employed a traditional wooden kingpost truss whereas the link span had the same light wrought-iron truss as the station. A significant innovation was the use of an elegant bowstring girder (or lenticular truss) to support the ends of this span in place of the cast-iron arcade used in the passenger station. This idea seems to have been pioneered by Andrews at Filey Station in 1846.

The original function of the area under the link span is uncertain.

The first Ordnance Survey plan of 1852 shows a single track but no passenger platform; possibly therefore it was an area for transhipping private carriages onto and off railway flat wagons - something quite common in the early days of railways. Both the goods shed and this roof were extended again in 1887, in close conformity with the original design.[8]

The original Malton goods shed was very awkwardly sited, squeezed in between the station and the coal depot and with sidings extending right across the station entrance. The hazard posed by engines shunting the sidings in front of the station was drawn to the attention of the Board of Trade by the local magistrates and an inspection took place in October 1857. By then, however, a new goods shed had been built and the dangers were much reduced by employing horses to shunt these lines instead.[9]

Malton's new goods shed, completed in April 1857, was much more ambitious than its predecessor. Designed by Thomas Prosser, the NER architect, it housed two platforms, for received and forwarded goods, and was wrapped round a central well lit by a glass roof. The design had no counterpart elsewhere on the NER but, stylistically, many of the details were picked up from Andrews' work - notably the conspicuous lunettes.[10] Despite teething problems with the roof, which soon had to be strengthened, it survived for almost a century, perishing by fire in July 1956 although its shell survived long after.

As well as stations, houses had to be provided for other railway staff. Originally, the most numerous grades were platelayers, responsible for track maintenance, and crossing keepers. In many cases the crossing was manned by a platelayer's family, who then occupied their gate cottage rent-free. Andrews' designs for gatehouses follow three patterns, exemplified by buildings at Strensall, Seamer and Howsham, the latter being the nearest point on the railway to Hudson's birthplace - indeed it was cited as a station on the opening day. These show variations on two themes: wall-panelling and the use of paired arched windows in the main gable, matched by arched chimneys. Though they appear small, the accommodation provided was good by the standards of contemporary rural housing: two bedrooms, a living room/kitchen and scullery. Unlike the station houses, these were not extended to meet family needs and, according to an 1862 survey, had to cope with typically a married couple and between three and six children.[11]

The York & North Midland Cottages adjoining Norton Road Crossing, Malton. Photo: Bill Fawcett.

The original Scarborough engine shed (below) with the enginemen's cottages on the left. The shed doorways have been enlarged from their original arched form, but the original doors have been retained. Photo: Ken Hoole collection.

Other platelayers and porters were housed in standard two-storey terraces, generally either two or three in a row. Two rooms up and two down, these provided the same accommodation as the gatehouses, albeit in a less picturesque fashion, and most survive.

An unusual variant was built opposite the level crossing to the east of Malton Station. The railway had diverted the existing roads to direct them onto a single crossing at the end of Malton Bridge and on some land left over they built a terrace of houses of two quite different styles and sizes: ordinary dwellings, two bays wide, and superior ones: taller and three bays wide with doorcases, clearly for superior staff. The 1862 survey reveals porters living in two of the smaller houses alongside an inspector and the Goods Yard Foreman in the larger ones. The coalyard at Malton also boasted an attractive house, intended for the coal agent and later occupied by the Assistant Stationmaster but with the weighing machine office built into the ground floor and characterised by a tripartite window. Scarborough's Falsgrave coalyard also featured such a house but to a less formal design.

Scarborough was the only place on the line originally to have an engine shed, a two-road building of typical Andrews' design, similar to that which survives at Richmond, though distinguished by the windows being set into recessed panels

With the introduction of block signalling onto the line in July 1873 there was a considerable increase in the number of signalmen employed, so in August work began on the construction of 18 cottages at a total cost of £3190-2-8 (£3190.13).[12][13] Built by William Bellerby, of York, the last ones were not finished until July 1875 so some staff had to wait two years for permanent accommodation, probably lodging with other railway families in the meantime. The new housing was to a neat standard design of Thomas Prosser and they were generally built in pairs. The contrast with their predecessors is best seen at Kirkham Abbey where they sit side-by-side on the riverbank. For these more spacious dwellings the weekly rent, in 1875, was two shillings and sixpence (12.5p), compared with two shillings (10p) for the old YNM ones.

Pickering had quite a fine ensemble of railway buildings, the principal ones executed in the local stone. Construction was delayed pending the reopening of the Whitby & Pickering with locomotives and so both station and goods shed contain more advanced features than at Malton and Scarborough. The station was a substantial affair with a trainshed whose hipped ends were carried by Filey-type bowstring girders. The station offices, though stylistically similar to those at Malton, are unassuming in the extreme, perhaps because of the very restricted site - squeezed between the Beck and the road. The goods shed displayed an evolution in plan, with a parallel railway track and roadway flanking a transhipment platform and the roof again extended beyond the building at one end to form a covered loading area. The single-road engine shed, though to a G. T. Andrews' design, appears to have been added later and was carried out in brick.[14] Curiously enough, the grandest of his designs in the town is a building which served for many years as a railway gasworks.

Early NER traction. Number 272, standing at the north end of Pickering Station, was built by the NER at Leeds in 1861 and scrapped in August 1888. Though a characteristic Fletcher locomotive, it may have been a renewal of a YNM Single. Photo: J.F. Mallon collection.

Chapter 4

Early Days

In order to pay its way, the Scarborough line needed not only to capture the existing traffic of the turnpikes and navigation but to generate much more. Stephenson's estimate for the scheme (including the Pickering Branch) had been a capital cost of £260,000, with running costs of £10,000 per annum set against a projected income of £42,425 made up of:

Passengers	£32,125
General Merchandise	2,500
Fish	1,600
Coals	4,700
Cereals	1,500

A surprising element in this is the overwhelming predominance of passenger revenue, and William Charles Copperthwaite, Earl Fitwilliam's Malton agent, estimated that, at current coaching fares, this would entail a threefold increase in passenger numbers from 24,920 (by road) in 1843 to 70,137.[1] The projected operating ratio (working expenses/revenue) of 24% was optimistic, something nearer 40% being typical of the period, but enabled Hudson to predict a return of over 10% on the capital invested.

The immediate profitability of the line is hard to judge, though within weeks of opening it saw its first 'monster excursion', from Tyneside. Extensive statistics are available for the year 1848 but the Scarborough (and Pickering) line revenues were lumped in with those of the YNM main line (York - Normanton) to give a total of £108,033 income from passengers or £125,613 for all revenue from passenger trains - i.e. adding in horses, parcels and mails. Known revenue and running costs are given in Appendix 1 and it seems safe to assume that the line was making a positive contribution to York & North Midland Railway profits.

This was not so with the Whitby & Pickering. Converting that line to locomotive working had entailed the reconstruction of all bridges and some earthworks, and it reopened in stages, finishing on 1 July 1847. The first full year of operation, 1848, brought gross receipts of just £11,194 for passengers and goods,

and the analysis in Appendix 1 suggests that shareholders would have been lucky to receive any return on the £341,478 capital invested.[2] This, however, is a short-term picture and overlooks both the strategic importance of that line to the YNM in terms of securing a monopoly in the area and the later expansion of holiday traffic.

Stephenson's capital cost estimate for the Scarborough line and Pickering Branch was, like many of its kind, wildly inaccurate. At £260,000, this came to £5,361 per mile compared with a known actual cost of £20,000 per mile for the original YNM[3]. Even allowing for the greater scale of bridges between York and Normanton, Hudson and his engineer had clearly chosen to understate the costs very considerably in order to persuade the shareholders to go ahead. In reality land purchases alone came to £111,633-9-1 while the outlay on Works had reached £339,995-14-2 by the end of June 1849.[4] Even that was not the end of the story for a major claim was still outstanding from Crawshaw, the contractor, in respect of the additional costs incurred in doubling the line.

Doubling involved widening substantial portions of the formation and all the wooden underbridges while keeping the line open for traffic on the original track, and Crawshaw justifiably argued that this was a more expensive procedure than the original construction. In 1847 he submitted a claim for £198,000, based on the original contract rates with the new quantities, but Hudson refused to settle and Crawshaw called in one of the Railway King's political opponents, the York lawyer, George Leeman, to represent him in further negotiations. Hudson resigned the YNM chair in May 1849, following the exposure of his shady deals and unjustified dividends on the York Newcastle & Berwick Railway (YNB), and the Directors were left to sort matters out, the dispute with Crawshaw being taken to arbitration in December.[5]

Both the YNM and YNB were weakened by Hudson's exposure, which brought about a crisis in the railway share market generally. The ultimate outcome of this was a defensive merger with the Leeds Northern Railway to form the North Eastern Railway (NER) from August 1854; this also embraced the humble Malton & Driffield Junction Railway, of which more later.

One indicator of the success of the Scarborough line was an immediate downturn in the fortunes of the Derwent Navigation. Anticipating the effects of competition, Earl Fitzwilliam had cut his tonnage rates on coal from 1s 8d (8.5p) to 1s 4d (6.5p) at the beginning of 1844. This failed to retain the traffic and he saw his profits slump from £4,145 in 1845 to £1,408 in 1846, the first full year of the railway's operation. Further rate cuts in concert with the Aire & Calder Navigation held some of the traffic - in 1852 17,120 tons of coal still went up the Derwent to Malton - but it had become almost unprofitable. By 1854 total receipts were down to £2,297, yielding a profit of just £600, with nothing in hand to cover future repairs.[6]

The newly-formed NER opened discussions which resulted in the sale of the navigation for the generous sum of £40,000, well in excess of its commercial value but worth paying in order to forestall possible incursions by other railways. As the NER was already a waterway owner and Parliament had passed anti-monopoly legislation to prevent one navigation from buying out another, the company could not purchase the Derwent Navigation outright. Instead it was sold to Trustees: Thomas Elliot Harrison, the NER's Engineer-in-Chief; Captain William O' Brien, its General Manager, and John James Gutch, its Solicitor.[7] The company then leased the navigation from them under an agreement dated 1 November 1855.

While the Derwent lingered on in a state of more-or-less benign neglect under the NER, the Foss Navigation, at the west end of the line, suffered a harsher fate. Opened in 1793, it comprised the canalised River Foss, from York to Strensall, and then a new cut across the fields to the head at Sheriff Hutton Bridge. The rural reach, upstream of York's Monk Bridge, was an early victim of the new railway and in 1853 John Cass Birkinshaw was invited to advise York Corporation, who were engaged in buying out the Foss Navigation Company to facilitate drainage improvement schemes.[8] Not surprisingly, Birkinshaw saw no future for the Foss. He reported that coal was sold at Flaxton and Strensall stations for 1/-6 (7.5p) per ton less than at the Canal Head. There was clearly no future for the navigation upstream of York but he saw no merit in retaining it within the City either. The artificially high level of the river led to drainage and flood problems and he advocated diverting the Foss into a culvert and demolishing the Walmgate stretch of the medieval City Walls to provide spoil to fill in the river bed. Fortunately, this idea aroused immense hostility and the navigation survives within the City Centre, now carrying a regular traffic in newsprint, which is more freight than remains on the railway.

The railway revolutionised passenger travel in the area. Instead

of the daily mail coach, the 1845 timetable provided 3 trains each way between York and Scarborough on weekdays, each with many times the capacity of the road coaches and a journey time cut from, at best, four hours to just two. As a result, the roads were abandoned by long-distance traffic and the York-Scarborough turnpike trust was wound up in 1865.

Bradshaw for March 1846 shows 4 down trains to Scarborough and 3 up to York, the latter supplemented by an early morning train on Mondays only which enabled people to reach London from Scarborough by early evening. The Whitby line was still being reconstructed so the mode of operation of the twice-daily horse-drawn coaches to and from Whitby is uncertain. The August timetable brought an enhanced Summer service to Scarborough, with five trains in each direction except on Sundays when there was only the mail train - accompanied, however, by numerous excursions. The Winter timetable (October to June) saw a return to four trains, with the Filey service, which began on 7 October, connecting at Seamer with three of these.

Regular locomotive working on the rebuilt Whitby line began from Pickering as far as Raindale Mill in August 1846 but the remainder was not ready until 1 July 1847, whereupon a Summer service of three trains each way was established on the branch, with, of course, just the single mail train on Sundays.

The Hudson crisis of 1849 brought about a reduction in the Scarborough line's Winter service to three trains, following the unusually tidy pattern exemplified by the June 1850 timetable given in Table 4.1. It was now possible to travel from York to Whitby in three hours and from Scarborough to Whitby, changing at Rillington, in just two and a half.

There were no dramatic developments in these services during the remaining life of the YNM or the early years of the NER other than the gradual abandonment of Rillington as the junction station for Whitby. By 1862 Malton was the connecting station for all trains except the 6 a.m. from York and 7.15 a.m. from Scarborough, and no other Scarborough trains called at Rillington, which was served by the Whitby Branch service instead. Express trains had also begun to appear: one down train completed the journey in 1 hour 40 minutes but pride of place went to the 10.15 a.m. from Scarborough to Leeds, which reached York in 1 hour 15 minutes and then waited there for a quarter hour (perhaps it could not be depended on to achieve this schedule) before proceeding to Leeds where it arrived at 1 p.m after a lengthy journey via Castleford. This heralded the main development in the line's regular schedule: a pattern of Leeds expresses culminating in today's Transpennine service.

Sundays continued to enjoy just one stopping train each way, leaving the day free for excursion traffic - which was both a valuable source of revenue and an operating nightmare. Holiday traffic took two forms. Cheap Sunday excursions provided a novel release for working people on their one free day but they did not yet have the time or money to take more extended holidays. Thus Scarborough's hotels and lodgings were frequented by a predominantly middle-class clientele, who normally stayed for multiples of a week, arriving and departing on Saturdays. They were catered for by the augmented Summer service and by a growing number of through trains from distant places on other railways, the most notable being the twentieth century's Scarborough Flier.

From its outset the line carried mail traffic, the company being obliged to under an Act of 1838, and this was conveyed by the first down train, reaching Scarborough originally at 9 a.m., and the last one up to York. So, for the first time the townspeople were able to enjoy a morning delivery of letters posted in London the previous day. The same train carried that day's London newspapers for the later breakfast tables of the holidaymakers.

The Post Office and YNM took a long time to agree rates for the mails. In April 1848 the well-known engineer, George Parker Bidder, was appointed an arbitrator on behalf of the railway but the issue was not resolved until October 1851 when an umpire, John Wilson Pattern M.P., settled a rate of £3-12-5 (£3.62) per day for all mails conveyed on the Scarborough and Whitby lines from 18 June 1848.[9]

In 1852, following improvements in the London-York service brought about by the opening of the Great Northern Railway's more direct route, the down mail was retimed to leave York at 6 a.m. in Summer, reaching Scarborough at 8, and this remained the pattern for over a decade. A dramatic improvement was made from 1 July 1865 when an express mail train was introduced, leaving York at 3.44 a.m. Stopping only at Malton it reached Scarborough at 5.10 and at last a breakfast-time delivery became possible for all. There continued to be a slow mail train, leaving at 5.45 a.m. and stopping at all stations.

The fast down mail was later retimed to leave York at 4.20 a.m. and its schedule then altered little until the First World War. At first it was intended to carry passengers only during the Summer, the service being maintained the rest of the year by a goods and mail train, but from the Autumn of 1892 it was extended to run all year round. As early as September 1857, the GPO requested accommodation for sorting staff in the Scarborough mail train, so that the mails could arrive sorted into the postmen's walks.[10] Originally this would have been provided within an ordinary vehicle but later a specialised sorting van was introduced. Although withdrawn during the First World War, this was reinstated in 1919 and ran until 1928. The mail train itself survived until 1980.

Other than excursions, rail travel in the early days was not cheap and regular travel lay beyond the reach of most working people. Table 4.2 shows the passenger fares charged by the YNM, the first-class being pitched just below the old mailcoach rate. The third-class fare, at 5/- (25p) single, was hardly intended to encourage mass travel at a time when the top wage for one of the company's own engine drivers was 7/- (35p) for a twelve-hour day.[11] Gladstone's Act of 1844 sought to redress this by compelling railways to run one train each weekday, stopping at all stations and conveying third-class passengers at 1d (0.4p) per mile: Bradshaw's *Government Class*. On the Scarborough line these *Parliamentary Trains* were the down mail from York and the first up train of the day.

Market tickets were available at a single fare (for the return journey) on specific trains and the YNM also ran a market train from Malton to York every Saturday morning, as well as another on alternate Thursdays in connection with York's Thursday Fortnight Fair.

Though freight traffic did not figure highly in the estimates of the promoters yet the Scarborough line had a major effect on local businesses, as witnessed by the coal and fish traffic.

Consider the case of Malton Gasworks. Opened in 1832, it drew coal via the Derwent Navigation from Silkstone Colliery on Earl Fitzwilliam's South Yorkshire estates.[12] Railway competition brought down the canal rates and it was not until 1866 that the Gas Company at last transferred their business to the railway, taking advantage of the accessibility of distant coalfields to sign a contract for 1867 with the New Brancepeth Colliery in West Durham. The following year they reverted to Silkstone coals at a price of 10/6 (52.5p) per ton delivered to Malton Station; in 1840 it had cost 8/6 (42.5p) per ton for transport alone plus a comparable amount for the coal itself. Thus, allowing 6d (2.5p) per ton for carriage from the station to the gasworks, the railway had brought about a reduction of 35% in raw material costs both through cheaper transport and bringing other suppliers into competition.

The coastal coal trade proved much less vulnerable. The decision to move Scarborough Gasworks from its original site down by the harbour to one adjoining the railway was only taken in 1873, while a significant sea trade in predominantly household coal continued, being reckoned at 17,000 tons in 1889.[13] This fell sharply, however, during the following decade and was down to just 1,470 tons in 1900.

At wayside stations the commission on coal sales was an important perquisite for the stationmaster but at Malton and Scarborough there were large depots with coal agents, most of whose income came from this commission. Although the original Scarborough coal depot was located at Falsgrave (also known as Washbeck coalyard), this was supplemented in 1851 by a very much larger depot built alongside the goods station.[14]

Fish was a distinctive feature of the line's outward freight. The regular carriage of fish from the Durham ports to Liverpool and Manchester had begun in 1841, with the completion of the YNM and Manchester & Leeds Railways. Scarborough followed and, though it was never a major fishing port, a special fish platform was established in the goods yard. Primitive forms of refrigeration, using ice, enabled the ports to consign fresh fish to the London markets leading to a boom in the fishing industry, particularly the herring fisheries. The importance of herring is shown in Table 4.3, where the enormous peak in traffic during September indicates that Scarborough was then one of the nearest ports to the great herring shoals making their Summer migration down the North Sea.[15]

Table 4.1. Passenger Service derived from Bradshaw June 1850

DOWN TRAINS TO SCARBOROUGH

York	7 am	12.00	5 pm
Haxby	7.07	12.07	5.07
Strensall	7.12	12.12	5.12
Flaxton	7.20	12.20	5.20
Barton	7.25	12.25	5.25
Kirkham Abbey	7.35	12.35	5.35
Castle Howard	7.39	12.39	5.39
Huttons Ambo	7.45	12.45	5.45
Malton	8.00	1 p.m	6.00
Rillington	8.10	1.10	6.10
Knapton	8.19	1.19	6.19
Heslerton	8.23	1.23	6.23
Sherburn	8.32	1.32	6.32
Ganton	8.36	1.36	6.36
Seamer	8.44 (a)	1.44 (b)	6.44
Scarborough	9.00	2.00	7.00
	c	d	e

Notes:
a - connection for Filey, arrive 9.25.
b - connection for Filey, arrive 2.25.
c - Mail Train runs every day 1, 2 & Govt class.
d - Mondays to Saturdays 1 & 2 class.
e - Mondays to Saturdays 1, 2, 3 class.

UP TRAINS FROM SCARBOROUGH

Scarborough	7.35am	12.15	4.05pm
Seamer	7.43	12.28	4.15
Ganton	7.52	12.36	4.26
Sherburn	7.55	12.40	4.35
Heslerton	8.03	12.48	4.38
Knapton	8.08	12.52	4.40
Rillington	8.15	1 p.m.	4.50
Malton	8.30	1.10	5.00
Huttons Ambo	8.38	1.18	5.07
Castle Howard	8.45	1.25	5.12
Kirkham Abbey	8.48	1.30	5.15
Barton	8.58	1.40	5.26
Flaxton	9.04	1.45	5.30
Strensall	9.10	1.50	5.38
Haxby	9.15	1.56	5.43
York	9.30	2.10	6.00
	a	b	c

Notes:
a - Mondays to Saturdays 1,2 & Govt class.
b - Mondays to Saturdays 1 & 2 class.
c - Mail Train runs every day. 1, 2 & 3 class weekdays. 1, 2 & Govt. Sundays.

DOWN TRAINS TO WHITBY

Rillington	8.18am	1.20pm.	6.10pm	8am
Marishes Road	8.25	1.30	6.15	8.10
Pickering	8.35	1.40	6.30	8.30
Levisham	8.45	1.55	6.45	8.45
Goathland	9.15	2.25	7.15	9.15
Grosmont	9.40	2.40	7.30	9.40
Sleights	9.50	3.02	7.52	9.50
Ruswarp	9.55	3.05	7.55	9.55
Whitby	10.00	3.10	8.00	10.00
	-Mondays to Saturdays -			*Sundays*

UP TRAINS FROM WHITBY

Whitby	6.30 a.m.	11.00	3.00 p.m.	
Ruswarp	6.35	11.05	3.05	
Sleights	6.40	11.10	3.10	
Grosmont	6.50	11.20	3.20	
Goathland	7.10	11.40	3.40	
Levisham	7.35	12.05	4.05	
Pickering	7.50	12.25	4.25	7.20 a.m.
Marishes Road	7.58	12.35	4.35	7.30
Rillington	8.08	12.50	4.50	7.40
	a	a	b	c

Notes:
a - Mondays to Saturdays
b - Runs all days
c - Sundays only

Table 4.2.   Fares on the Scarborough and Whitby lines in July 1848

From York to:	First		Second		Third Class	
Haxby	1/-	*(5)*	9d	*(3.75)*	6d	*(2.5)*
Strensall	1/6	*(7.5)*	1/-	*(5)*	9d	*(3.75)*
Flaxton	2/-	*(10)*	1/6	*(7.5)*	1/-	*(5)*
Barton	2/6	*(12.5)*	2/-	*(10)*	1/6	*(7.5)*
Kirkham Abbey	3/6	*(17.5)*	2/6	*(12.5)*	2/-	*(10)*
Castle Howard	3/6	*(17.5)*	2/6	*(12.5)*	2/-	*(10)*
Huttons Ambo	4/-	*(20)*	3/-	*(15)*	2/3	*(11.25)*
Malton	5/-	*(25)*	3/6	*(17.5)*	2/6	*(12.5)*
Rillington	6/-	*(30)*	4/-	*(20)*	3/-	*(15)*
Knapton	6/6	*(32.5)*	4/6	*(22.5)*	3/-	*(15)*
Heslerton	6/6	*(32.5)*	4/6	*(22.5)*	3/6	*(17.5)*
Sherburn	7/6	*(37.5)*	5/6	*(27.5)*	4/-	*(20)*
Ganton	8/-	*(40)*	5/6	*(27.5)*	4/-	*(20)*
Seamer	9/-	*(45)*	6/6	*(32.5)*	4/6	*(22.5)*
Scarborough	10/-	*(50)*	7/-	*(35)*	5/-	*(25)*
Pickering	8/-	*(40)*	5/6	*(27.5)*	4/-	*(20)*
Whitby	12/-	*(60)*	9/6	*(47.5)*	7/-	*(35)*

Fares in pence quoted in brackets

The fares were based on a tariff of 3d/mile (1.2p) first class, 2d (0.8p) second class and 1.5d (0.6p) third class, generally rounded down to a multiple of 3d. Day return fares were available at 1.5 times the single fare, except on Sundays. Day tickets issued on Saturdays could be used to return the following Monday: an early form of Weekend Return.

Table 4.3.   Monthly Revenue from fish consigned at Scarborough during 1870

January	£80-0-4	July	£183-15-5
February	17-15-9	August	680-19-7
March	11-1-1	September	1731-11-1
April	83-17-10	October	800-17-11
May	16-13-2	November	102-12-10
June	47-12-0	December	40-1-11

*The earliest known view of the Scarborough line in York, from a photograph in the Evelyn Collection of the Yorkshire Architectural &
York Archaeological Society. The whereabouts of the original painting are unknown. It shows the view from Bootham across the Ouse
towards the site of the present station. The only hint of the river is the sail of a barge. On the right the Scarborough line crosses Marygate
Ings on a low brick viaduct; behind are the YNM waterworks and the bridge carrying Thief Lane.*

NER Class P3 heading the pickup goods through Malton Station in the nineteen-fifities. In the background is Malton signalbox. The up platform originally ended where the platform steps back. Photo: J. F. Mallon.

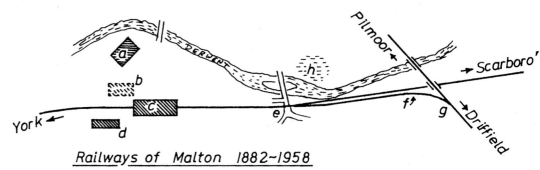

Railways of Malton 1882~1958

a ~ Goods Station   b ~ Site of first Goods Station
c ~ Passenger Station   d ~ Engine Shed
f ~ Site of Norton Town Jc.   g ~ Scarboro' Road Jc.
e ~ Malton East Jc.   h ~ Gasworks

The Railways of Malton: 1882-1958.

Chapter 5

All Change at York, Malton & Scarborough

The eighteen-fifties saw Malton transformed into a junction by the opening of a line to the west, up Ryedale, and another south-east across the Wolds to Driffield. Both served agricultural districts with little potential for traffic development. The Malton and Driffield Junction (MDJ) was promoted by local landowners, Lord Morpeth (of Castle Howard) being chairman, but also received George Hudson's endorsement with a promise of £40,000 from the YNM. It got its Act in 1846 and construction brought back two figures from the building of the Scarborough line: John Cass Birkinshaw, as consulting engineer, and Alfred Dickens, still resident in Malton, to supervise the work. In the event, Birkinshaw left in 1849 and Dickens was left to complete the line, including a mile-long tunnel through the Wolds at Burdale.

Thomas Cabry was the YNM Engineer, in charge of its civil engineering and locomotive departments, in which capacity he directed, and probably indeed drove, the inaugural train on the Scarborough line. Asked his opinion of the MDJ by a committee of YNM shareholders anxious about their investment, he replied simply and accurately "It will never pay"; it later turned out to be one of the most unprofitable lines on the NER system. Nonetheless the company was so bound up with the YNM and the Ryedale line that it was included in the amalgamation which formed the North Eastern Railway. As a result, William Charles Copperthwaite, a director of the MDJ, joined the North Eastern Board to provide a local voice. He also founded a railway dynasty: his son, Harold, trained as a civil engineer and eventually succeeded to Cabry's post as NER Southern Division Engineer while his grandson, Ralph, became the manager of the company's Darlington Works.

The Malton & Driffield opened formally on 19 May 1853 (regular traffic began on 1 June) from a junction a quarter mile east of Norton level crossing and also provided the connecting link for the Ryedale (or Thirsk & Malton) line which opened at the same time.[1] This branch, from Malton to Pilmoor on the East Coast Main Line, had been promoted by the York Newcastle & Berwick Railway during the heady days of Hudson. After his fall they unwillingly found themselves legally obliged to proceed with construction despite its poor financial prospects.

Though neither branch did much for the traffic or revenues of the Scarborough line, both offered useful alternative routes to the Coast for holiday trains at a time when the main line through York was badly congested. The Ryedale line was particularly helpful in enabling Scarborough trains from Glasgow, Edinburgh and Tyneside to bypass York, though working was complicated by the junction layout at Malton. Heading south, these trains crossed a bridge over the Scarborough line and then dropped at 1 in 55 down to the Driffield branch, continuing along it until they had cleared the junction. A Malton pilot engine then coupled onto the rear and drew the train into the station, where it reversed again and was soon heading under the Ryedale line towards Scarborough. A grandstand view of all this was obtained from vehicles held up at Norton Road level crossing.

Malton's new role as a junction required an expansion of the station and other facilities.[2] In July 1853 Cabry got his directors' approval to build a two-road engine shed behind the station, to house four locomotives. This was probably nearing completion by the following March when the company ordered a new water tank and two water cranes. Passengers changing trains were catered for by refreshment rooms added in 1855 as a two-storey block matching, though not identical to, the stationmaster's villa and having staff accommodation on the upper floor.

A major station remodelling was delayed until 1862. By then Malton had become the connecting station for most Whitby trains, instead of Rillington, and in August the NER Board confirmed this policy, having already begun some of the changes needed to fit the station for this role.[3]

The most pressing need was for a separate platform to handle Whitby trains, and this was met by extending the down (Scarborough) platform at its east end and forming a new bay on its north face. The platform was also widened, to improve circulation, the requisite space being gained by removing the original down line. The former up line to York became the new down line to Scarborough, and a new up line was provided behind the rear wall of the trainshed with the old up platform extended through that wall to serve it. The columns at either end

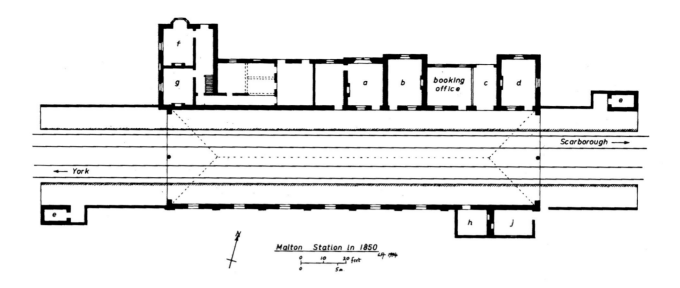

Ground Plan of Malton Station in 1850; a, b, d, h & j are waiting rooms, c is the booking hall & station entrance, e are water towers with a men's urinal in the base, f is the sitting - room of the stationmaster's house, g is the stationmaster's kitchen . Bill Fawcett.

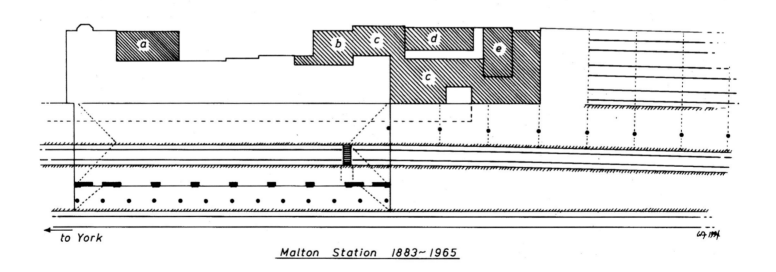

Ground plan of Malton Station from 1883 to 1965 with extensions to the original building denoted by shading: a is an extension of the Stationmaster's House. b is an extension to the station offices. c are the refreshment rooms. e is the toilet. Drawing: Bill Fawcett.

of the station roof were now found to be in the way and so they were simply removed and their capitals tied up to the end girders with iron rods; eventually lattice girders were substituted instead. Thomas Prosser, the NER architect, provided a characteristically handsome verandah roof for the new up platform.

The engine shed was already proving too small and, after toying with the idea of building a new one, the NER extended it in 1867, adding an extra four bays at each end.[4]

For a time many quite busy NER stations relied on a sleeper crossing at the platform ends to gain access across the tracks. The Board of Trade was not happy with this and by the late eighteen-sixties footbridges began to appear. Malton, however, acquired an almost unique link between its platforms in the form of a retractable trolley bridge, suitably interlocked with the signals. When not required this was drawn back into a recess below the up platform.

The final developments came in the early eighteen-eighties. To relieve congestion, the NER moved the junction with the Driffield line back to the level crossing, providing an extra pair of tracks between there and the site of the original Norton Town Junction. The station's down platform was again extended and in 1883 was provided with what amounted to a miniature trainshed over the Whitby bay and two adjoining carriage sidings. Very much in the style of the then NER Chief Architect, William Bell, it was covered with ridge and furrow roofing which continued as a verandah up to the original trainshed.

During the early decades of the Scarborough Branch the most serious obstacles to effective working lay at the west end, in congestion at York and the absence of a direct route from York to Leeds. The latter problem vanished in 1869 with the opening of two lines: the Church Fenton-Micklefield cut-off, which gave direct access from York onto the old Leeds & Selby route, and an extension through Leeds linking with the London & North Western and Midland Railways and serving a new station. This shortened the distance from 33 to 25.5 miles and cut the journey time of the best Leeds-Scarborough expresses over this stretch from 75 minutes in 1862 to 40 minutes a decade later.

York took longer to sort out, the main problem being the location of both passenger and goods stations on a cramped site within the medieval city walls. The first improvement came in 1845

when, shortly before the opening of the Scarborough line, Hudson leased the Great North of England Railway (GNE), the YNM's partner in York Station. This enabled him to close the YNM coal depot, adjoining the station, and transfer the business to an enlarged GNE depot, outside the city walls. On the site vacated was built an extension to the passenger station. The earthen bank of the city defences was cut back and retained by a brick wall, supporting one side of a trainshed which sheltered two narrow platforms. As well as adding these *Scarborough Bays* the company lengthened the two original platforms and added a further track on the far side of the station, giving five platform faces in all. The bottleneck of the station throat was eased by forming a second arch through the city wall and diverting onto its two new tracks all traffic for the goods station. Through freight traffic was assisted by building a loop between the Normanton and Darlington lines but this did nothing to ease workings onto the Scarborough line, which still entailed a reversal for passenger and freight trains from York and the south.

While all this provided valuable relief, the long-term solution was to replace the terminus with a through station outside the straightjacket of York's defences. In its early years the NER had other priorities and, despite obtaining an Act for this station and associated lines in 1866, financial worries and the heavy investment at Leeds caused the scheme to be deferred. It was revived in 1871 and the present passenger station opened 6 years later, the largest in the world at that time and still well able, with the provision of further through platforms, to meet today's needs.

What York got was not just a new passenger station but almost a complete replacement of its railway infrastructure: goods station, coal depot and engine sheds. Much of this sprawled across the site of the Scarborough line and operation must have been quite awkward during the construction period. The Ouse Bridge was rebuilt, Thief Lane realigned and renamed Leeman Road, in honour of the NER chairman, and the level of the line was raised 4 feet (1.2m) to bring it up to that of the new station, which was formally opened on 25 June 1877. The earliest train on which passengers were booked that day was the 5.30 a.m. to Scarborough, consequently there were many more passengers than usual, travelling just to Haxby in order to claim they had been on the first train.

Once all this work at York had been completed, the NER felt able to embark on major improvements at Scarborough:

transforming the passenger station and replacing the engine shed with something more spacious.

The enlargement of Scarborough Station had already been progressing piecemeal for years in order to meet the ever-growing demands of the holiday traffic. The first major scheme followed a report commissioned from the NER's Engineer-in-Chief, Thomas Elliot Harrison, towards the end of 1856.[5] As a result of this, a long excursion platform, the present No. 1, was provided at the south end of the station with its own cabstand opening onto Westborough and the whole area covered with a roof very similar to that of the original trainshed. Work on the platform and tracks was approved in January 1857 but there was then a delay of two years before the designs of their architect, Thomas Prosser, were finally sanctioned.[6]

The work was largely completed for the 1859 Summer season and comprised the roof over platform 1 (D in plan on page 49), the cabstand (C), an arcaded screen wall to Westborough and lengthening the original trainshed roof by two bays (B), supported at the rear by a pair of columns rather than an extension of the trainshed wall. No extra waiting rooms were built, instead the extensive roof sheltered a circulating area, where excursion passengers queued for their return trains. Additional toilets were provided, together with a large parcels and left-luggage office at the terminal end of platform 1 (a in plan on page 49). At some stage, but not apparently as a part of the original scheme, a second bay platform, the present No. 2, was added while the original arrival platform (now No. 3) was widened, over the site of the adjoining track, to improve access to the waiting and refreshment rooms. Since there was a desperate shortage of carriage sidings at Scarborough the original departure platform was removed and a siding took its place. Thus the station retained the same number of platforms but the new *Middle Dock* (platform 2) was much longer than its predecessor.

By the eighteen-seventies Scarborough station was again under heavy pressure from the growth in holiday traffic while the system was about to be augmented by a coastal line to Whitby (the Scarborough & Whitby Railway was begun in 1872 although it did not open until 1885) and the NER's Forge Valley Line, from Seamer to Pickering, which opened on 1 May 1882. Coupled with the local complaints recounted in the next chapter, these prompted a major review of facilities.

Once more, Harrison was called on to prepare a solution to the traffic problems, caused largely by the restricted station site and the shortage of carriage sidings. One option considered was relocating the goods station and coalyard. Two alternative sites were proposed, one at the Falsgrave coal depot and the other on NER-owned land on the opposite side of Westwood from the station.[7] The latter was probably rejected because of cost; it would have entailed a long skew bridge under Westwood and extensive earthworks to make that steeply-sloping site up to the required level. Instead, the company embarked on a partial realignment and extension of platforms 1 and 2, together with major improvements to the station facilities. In the course of this, platform 1 became virtually an independent excursion station with its own separate waiting rooms and booking office.

By May 1878 the necessary platform realignment and track alterations had been carried out, the whole station had been resignalled and next month the NER received Board of Trade approval for this, just in time for the Summer traffic.[8] The following January work started on a low-level roof over platforms 2 and 3, which was completed in mid August.[9] There was then a pause in developments at the station while the rest of the railway infrastructure was sorted out, chiefly the provision of a long-overdue new engine shed and an additional running line, the Down Independent, to link it with the station.

The second phase of work at the station was to improve the excursion facilities. Platform 1 had already been extended well outside its trainshed, so that today it can hold a 13 coach train. In December 1882 work began on extending the platform roof to match and building excursion waiting rooms and a ticket office (c-e in plan on page 49).[10] These were provided with two access routes from Westborough: a covered pedestrian ramp and a cab ramp. Designed by the current NER architect, William Bell, the work was meticulously executed using the warm, buff local brick (also adopted for York Station). The extension was given a handsome arcaded frontage to Westborough, continued along the cab ramp, and the whole was roofed in by a major extension to the 1859 trainshed (EFH) albeit in a mixture of styles - some matching the earlier roof but the final stretch of platform 1 having a verandah (G) similar to that at Malton; the roof contractors were the well-known Derby ironfounders, Handysides.

Work on the excursion platforms was virtually finished by the end of July 1883 so the NER then felt able to proceed with the

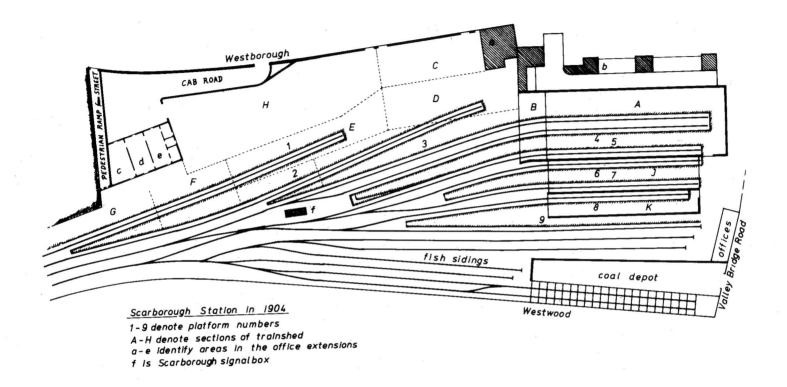

Scarborough Station in 1904
1-9 denote platform numbers
A-H denote sections of trainshed
a-e identify areas in the office extensions
f is Scarborough signalbox

Ground Plan of Scarborough Station in 1904 with extensions to the original offices denoted by shading: A is the original trainshed B is the two-bay extension of 1859 J is the original link span, as lengthened K is the former goods shed, as lengthened, b are the pavilions and cabshelter, c-e are the excursion waiting rooms and booking office. Bill Fawcett.

A general view of Scarborough Station on 23 April 1959. The station signalbox (just called Scarborough) can be seen at the end of platforms 4 and 5, while the four high-level roof bays in front of the 1883 excursion waiting rooms are on the left. Photo: Ken Hoole.

Scarborough Station rooftops in 1970, showing how the south pavilion and clocktower were built in front of the original office range. In the background is the Pavilion Hotel, then about to celebrate its centenary, since demolished. Photo: Bill Fawcett.

final phase, improving the facilities within the original station and sorting out the mess into which its once-dignified frontage had disintegrated, G.T. Andrews' portico having been replaced in 1870 by a more functional but unsightly cantilevered glass awning. William Bell came up with a brilliant solution. The awning was despatched to Malton Station and in its place he provided three pedimented pavilions, whose detailing matches Andrews' work so well that most people assume them to be original. The end pavilions housed the extensive toilets required and between them he strung light, glazed roofs to shelter the cabstands.[11] Finally, to restore the station's impact on the late-Victorian skyline, he topped the central pavilion with a tall, bulbous, almost baroque clocktower.

Despite all this investment, the station still had only three platforms. More were needed to cope with the Pickering and Whitby services but could only be accommodated by resiting either the station carriage sidings or the goods station. Seeing that expansion within the town centre was now impractical, the NER had been purchasing land in the Weaponess Valley, particularly on the west side of the line, adjoining Seamer Road. By 1875 they owned a number of fields in that area but they were not the first to begin the industrialisation of the Valley. There were brickworks on the opposite side of the road but, more dramatically, in 1873 Scarborough Gas Company began building a new works there, on the east side of the line, having originally been located in Quay Street where their coal came in by sea.[12]

By 1878 the NER was ready to build a new engine shed. The original two-road shed had long been inadequate and most of the engines must have been stabled out of doors. The actual design was not agreed until the following year, probably because of concern about the suitability of the Seamer Road site. The NER favoured square roundhouses, square sheds with typically 20 roads radiating from a central turntable, but the restricted depth of this site meant they could not have a full roundhouse. Instead they had a half one with 13 roads, including the two entrance lines, served by a 44 ft 8 inch (14.1m) turntable. Although the new locomotive yard was brought partly into use during the Autumn of 1880, the building was not completed until September 1881.[13] While this was going on, the Washbeck Viaduct was rebuilt and widened to carry four tracks including an independent running line linking the station with the new shed.

The old engine shed was converted into an additional goods shed

but the goods station and the main coal depot remained alongside the terminus, inhibiting further expansion there. The stables for the company's horses were also on that site, since they were principally used for the local collection and delivery of goods, but some relief was provided from October 1883 with the completion of new stables at Sherwood Street, an area then being developed for housing.[14] This cleared the way, not for more passenger platforms but a final extension of the old goods shed four years later.

Meanwhile, the new engine shed soon proved inadequate, and in June 1888 the directors authorised an additional eight-road straight shed to house 24 engines. Completed in 1890, this was sited to the south of its predecessor; the space between them being developed as the locomotive yard, originally with a 50 feet (14.2m) diameter turntable supplied by J. Butler for £305. As locomotives developed, so they regularly outgrew their turntables and in 1924 this was replaced by a 60 feet (17.4m) one just in time for the Summer season. Purchased from Cowans Sheldon, of Carlisle, in 1916 for £964 16s 7d (£964.66) this had originally been earmarked for Goole. It in turn was too short to handle the Pacific locomotives of a later era and had outriggers fitted in May 1934 in an attempt to ease the problem of balancing larger locomotives. It was not until 14 years after the end of regular steam workings that a 70 feet (19.9m) turntable was finally installed in connection with the *Scarborough Spa Express* steam-hauled excursions.

The problem of carriage stabling, for excursion trains, was tackled in stages. Between the new Washbeck bridge and Belgrave Terrace (formerly Love Lane) bridge, two sidings were added on the up side together with an independent running line. The NER's *Additional Powers* Act of 1882 provided for further expansion on that side at the other end of the Washbeck bridge, opposite the engine shed, but this was conditional on the consent of Dr. John Cass Smart since the site included the grounds of his villa.[15] In the event, development was limited to the provision of the five Gasworks Up sidings. Despite their name these were not originally linked to the track leading into the gasworks and served as carriage sidings.[16]

By 1890, a further three carriage sidings had appeared on the down side of the line but the major development was in Summer 1898 when the extended Gasworks Down Sidings were opened. These provided a well-organised block of nine sidings accessed

A reboilered McDonnell Class 38 Number 112 standing under the low-level roof at the head of platform 2 apparently around the turn of the century. There is a good view through the excursion trainshed of 1859 to cabs waiting under the 1883 cabstand roof.
Photo: Leslie Good (photographer) Laurie Ward collection.

Another McDonnell Class 38 waiting to leave platform 3 at Scarborough with a train for York, possibly during the eighteen-nineties, with the excursion platforms 1 and 2 in the background.
Photo: Laurie Ward collection.

by an extension of the Down Independent, although the two longest sidings were still at Gasworks Up - with standage of 352 and 278 yards (322m and 254m), compared with typically 225 yards (206m) at Gasworks Down. At the same time a link was made between the gasworks and the Up Sidings to facilitate their use for coal traffic.[17]

The opening in 1885 of the Scarborough and Whitby Railway, worked from the outset by the NER and purchased by it in 1898, added an extra complication to operations at Scarborough. The line came in from the north past a large parcel of land at Gallows Close, originally intended for a terminus. It then passed through a tunnel under Falsgrave Road, joining the NER at the end of platform 1 but facing in the wrong direction so that Whitby trains had to reverse into and out of the station, a situation exacerbated by their use of platforms 4 and 5, on the opposite side of the main lines. These platforms were built on the site of the former carriage sidings within the original station and this involved two alterations to the trainshed roof. One of the end columns was taken out and its capital trussed up to the roof, as at Malton, while the two columns provided in 1859 to extend the rear wall of the building were replaced by a curving masonry wall, to provide clearance for the platform 5 track.

Whatever its operational problems, the Whitby Branch brought one important compensation. The NER purchased the Gallows Close site from the Scarborough & Whitby Company, despite the opposition of that line's contractor and principal stockholder, John (Paddy) Waddell, who wished to build an independent goods depot there. The NER used it to resite its goods depot instead and this opened for traffic on 13 June 1899, although construction of a new goods shed there did not begin until almost two years later, being completed in June 1902[18] The new building was a spacious contrast to its predecessor, with separate benches (i.e. platforms) for *forward* and *received* traffic, each 234 feet (71m) long.

So in 1902 the old goods shed at last became redundant and could be absorbed into the passenger station. Its end wall was opened out and a further four platforms were provided, two there (8 and 9) and two under the adjoining G.T. Andrews' link roof (6 and 7). This did nothing to solve the problem of excursion trains; the new platforms were quite short and only platform 1 could handle really long trains. The North Eastern

did not lack land; it still owned the site first proposed for the Scarborough terminus on the south side of Westwood but had no ready means of access.[19] The development of large villas further along that side of Westwood effectively stopped them from widening the station throat, so the only space accessible for further development close to the town centre was the original engine shed site adjoining Londesborough Road. The solution adopted was to build an excursion station there, completely separate from the existing station, which was renamed Scarborough Central.

No longer needed for goods traffic, the 1845 engine shed was demolished, though the nearby Locomotive Cottages survived, and Washbeck Excursion Station (later renamed Londesborough Road) took its place, while further carriage sidings to accommodate up to ten trains were provided alongside the Whitby line at Northstead together with a 60 feet (18.3m) turntable. Despite being a very long way beyond Gallows Close, these sidings were generally known by that name.

The new station opened on 8 June 1908 and provided one long through platform and a bay, together with a spacious circulating area covered by a light, fully glazed roof.[20] Excursion trains could now unload their passengers and then proceed straight on through the tunnel to Gallows Close Carriage Sidings, where facilities were provided to coal and water engines, as well as turn them. So at very busy times they need not visit the engine shed at all, unless requiring more extensive maintenance. These sidings could also handle much longer trains than their predecessors: typically 15 British Railways Mark 1 carriages compared with 10 at most of the Gasworks Down Sidings. With this development, the hectic growth of Scarborough's railway infrastructure was at an end and, with modest improvements, it would serve in this form until the nineteen-sixties.

Scarborough Station frontage in 1970, with a typical summertime clutter of traffic in the forecourt. Photo: Bill Fawcett.

Scarborough's former Sherwood Street Stable. The 1884 block with the beam for the sack hoist. It later became an LNER road motor depot. Photo: Bill Fawcett.

The trolley bridge between the platforms at Malton Station in July 1955. Photo courtesy of C. J. B. Sanderson.

A Fletcher BTP Number 954 shunting the goods yard at Scarborough Station, apparently during the late eighteen-eighties. In the background can be seen the trainshed of platforms 1 and 2, together with the low-level awning over platform 3. The engine has acquired an elegant McDonnell chimney in place of its original stovepipe, but is otherwise largely in its original condition. Photo: J. F. Mallon collection.

The speedy singles. T. W. Worsdell Class I Number 1528 leaving Scarborough in 1909 with a typical train of David Bain's clerestory carriages. Photo: K. L. Taylor collection.

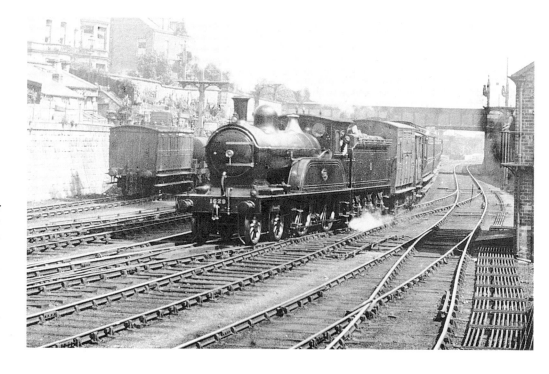

Class M1 Number 1629 heading out of Scarborough. On the right is the original Falsgrave signalbox, opened in 1873 and replaced by a very much larger structure on the opposite side of the line on 26 April 1908. The leading vehicle is a horsebox followed by a perishables van, possibly conveying fish. Photo: Laurie Ward collection.

Chapter 6

Traffic and Train Services 1872–1914

By 1872, with the opening of a direct route from York to Leeds, the regular passenger services had reached a level of maturity. From then up to 1914 there were major improvements in the speed and frequency of services but no dramatic change in the basic pattern. The First World War reversed this progress and things were only just getting back to normal by 1 January 1923, when the NER became the major partner in a new London & North Eastern Railway under the grouping scheme imposed by Parliament.

The most conspicuous development in scheduled services up to 1914 was the improvement in the Scarborough-Leeds expresses.[1] This reflected changes in the town's role as a resort. The existence of the railway, combined with the expansion of the middle-classes in the industrial towns of Northern England, had prompted a dramatic growth in the number of holidays being taken in the town, coupled with a growth in population from 10,048 in 1841 to 38,161 by 1901. The speeding up of services made possible a new type of being: the commuter, a West Riding businessman who transferred his home to Scarborough for the Summer and travelled daily by train into the office seventy miles away.

By 1872 it was already possible to commute daily; even in Winter one could leave Scarborough at 8.20 a.m., reaching Leeds at 10.15, and returning at 5 p.m. to reach home at 7.05; this entailed timings of 70 minutes up (with a stop at Malton) and 75 minutes down (stopping at Malton and Seamer) over the Scarborough line. By the eighteen-eighties the pattern had not changed much although the fastest time for the 42 miles had nudged down to 65 minutes.

From 1891 the NER management received a shake-up with the appointment of George Stegmann Gibb as general manager in place of the veteran Henry Tennant, whose railway career dated back almost a half century to the Brandling Junction Railway on Tyneside. One of Gibb's first reforms was the abolition of the Second Class, whose patronage had declined to insignificant levels thanks to improvements in the quality of Third Class travel and the opening up of express services to all classes. At this time North Eastern expresses were still operated by six-wheeled coaches, with the surviving four-wheelers no doubt pressed into service for excursion use. In 1895 York Carriage Works embarked on a major programme of new construction, bringing the first bogie vehicles into general use on the system. The Leeds-Scarborough expresses were an early recipient of David Bain's handsome clerestory carriages. By 1899 these were made up of 1st/3rd class composites with lavatories accessible from the majority of compartments but without vestibule connections between the carriages.[2]

By the Summer of 1899 the fastest down train was doing the journey from Leeds to Scarborough in 1 hour 45 minutes, with a non-stop run of 55 minutes from York, while one up train made this stage in 50 minutes. This was soon to be eclipsed, however. On 1 June 1900 the North Eastern inaugurated a non-stop Summer express which slashed the time for the 67.5 miles from Leeds to 75 minutes. The head of the NER Traffic Department, the Superintendent of the Line, Philip Burtt, was on the inaugural train, together with the District Superintendent, Mr. Harper, and must have been disappointed that signal checks between Leeds and York caused it to arrive one minute late despite a heroic run from York to Scarborough in 42.5 minutes, virtually a 60mph average despite the speed restrictions on the bends between Barton Hill and Malton.

This train provided an ideal vehicle for T. W. Worsdell's Class J 4-2-2 express locomotives. Introduced only a decade earlier these had proved themselves fast runners on the East Coast Main Line but, like Stirling's famous Great Northern Singles, were soon displaced as trains got heavier. By contrast they were really at home with the *Scarborough Limited* and a light load of typically four coaches, approximately 110 tons. The schedule allowed about 27 minutes from Leeds to York, where they had to slow down to 10 mph while passing through the station, then 48 minutes to Scarborough. This entailed fast running wherever possible, notably down the bank from Micklefield to Church Fenton and along the straight and level stretch from Rillington to Ganton. As one example, Number 1524 was recorded completing the journey one and a half minutes early with speeds of 77.5 mph down Micklefield Bank and 73.7 mph at Ganton, while in 1913 Cecil J. Allen logged Number 1523 on a three coach train doing 85 mph down Micklefield Bank.[3] The businessmen may have found this a mixed blessing as they lurched through Micklefield Junction on switches which were not designed to provide a smooth ride above about 40 mph.

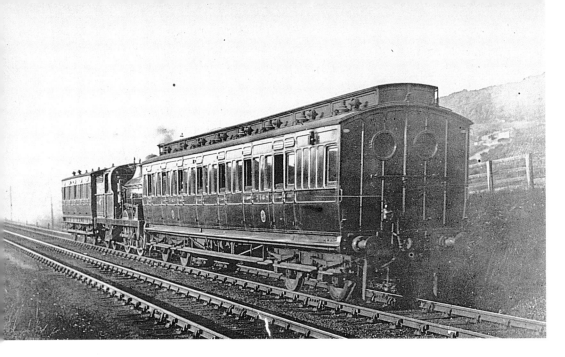

An autotrain, similar to that used between York and Strensall, operating in the Weaponess Valley between Scarborough and Seamer. Note the porthole windows of the driver's compartment and the six-wheeled carriage added behind the locomotive.
Photo: J. F. Mallon collection.

The early LNER period, yet still a typically North Eastern scene just east of Kirkham Abbey as D22 (NER Class F) Number 1541 heads towards Scarborough. The train is made up of NER carriages except for the leading vehicle, which appears to be an East Coast Joint Stock luggage brake.
Photo: J. F. Mallon collection.

The popularity of the *Scarborough Limited* (an unofficial title) in its first season led a deputation of Leeds businessmen to attend the NER Board with a request that it be extended to run all year round. The company felt there would not be enough Winter traffic to justify this and so it continued to run in the Summer only. It was, however, extended through from Bradford with, by 1914, a departure time of 4.45 p.m. from the Midland station (Forster Square) and 5.13 from Leeds. In the up direction the schedule was 5 minutes slower, with an 8.20 a.m. departure from Scarborough reaching Leeds at 9.40 and Bradford at 10.10.

The other prestigious express service was the *Scarborough Flier* from Kings Cross, which originated in the through trains introduced in 1901, although the name was not used officially until 1927. For many years the fastest journey to Scarborough was provided by the 10 a.m. from Kings Cross, which became famous as the Flying Scotsman. In 1853 this connected at York to provide a 6.05 p.m. arrival at Scarborough, while the 9.15 a.m. from Scarborough provided a 7.10 p.m. arrival at Kings Cross (or 10 p.m. at Euston); in addition there were overnight services but not, of course, sleepers. By 1862 Scarborough could be reached at 4.45 p.m. This was by the original Doncaster-York route via Knottingley but in January 1871 the NER opened a more direct line through Selby which speeded up the main line service so that in 1886 the Scarborough arrival was 3.30, despite a 35 minutes wait for the connection at York; in the reverse direction, the 11 a.m. from Scarborough gave a 5 p.m. arrival in London.

Although there had already been through carriages on other trains, 1901 brought the first regular through train, a Summer service leaving Kings Cross at 11.30 a.m. and reaching Scarborough at 4.40 p.m., with timings of 2.55 p.m. departure and 8.30 p.m. arrival in the up direction. A faster journey could still be had by other trains, changing at York, but the convenience of a through service for holidaymakers with luggage more than made up for this. By 1914 it was running on Fridays and Saturdays only, while a faster daily service was provided by a Luncheon Car Express leaving London at 1.05 p.m. and reaching Scarborough at 5.54. Both trains were notionally non-stop through York but in reality halted there to change engines.

While the local services were not neglected by the North Eastern, little could be done to speed up trains which stopped at 14 intermediate stations; by 1914 there were five each way which called at all stations, with a best time of 1 hour 37 minutes. In addition, the once solitary Sunday train had swelled out to a Summer schedule of four down trains and five up, three of each being expresses.

The company also had an eye to the development of suburban traffic into York and in 1902 considered installing a turntable at Strensall so that they could use it as a terminus for additional local trains. Though this was not done, in 1904 the NER successfully experimented with autocars (push-&-pull trains) at the Hartlepools and subsequently introduced a modest service of these from York as far as Strensall and, in some cases, Flaxton.[4]

The Summer brought exotic colours into the line's regular trains as they were augmented by through coaches from distant towns. Taking the Summer of 1890 as an example, there were Midland carriages from Bristol, Sheffield, Leicester and St. Pancras, Great Northern from Nottingham and Leicester, Lancashire & Yorkshire from Liverpool and Manchester, and London & North Western from Liverpool, Leamington and Oxford, as well as regular trains worked from Sheffield by the Manchester Sheffield & Lincolnshire (MS & L, later Great Central) Railway.[5] Some of the routes may now seem rather unexpected, thus the LNWR's Oxford train ran over that company's branch line to Bletchley, up their main line to Northampton and then via Market Harborough to Melton Mowbray, whence the GN & LNW Joint Line brought it to Newark and the East Coast Main Line.

Nearly all the through carriages were marshalled into the Scarborough trains at York, and increased loadings meant that some trains had to be duplicated. In August 1883, for instance, the 11 a.m. express from Scarborough to Leeds was duplicated, with the first portion comprising Midland carriages and permitted to leave a few minutes before the advertised departure time.[6] At York, which then had only two through platforms, it ran into the up platform, then number 4, while the second portion, the actual Leeds express following a few minutes later, ran through the station on the centre roads and then set back into platform 3, one of the west end bays.

As traffic grew, many of these holiday trains came to be worked separately and hauled throughout by a locomotive from the originating company. The Scarborough traffic was worth competing for. Thus when the MS & L opened its extension to London and became the Great Central it came into rivalry with the Midland for traffic from Leicester and Nottingham, initiating a through train from Marylebone Station to Scarborough in the summer of 1901.[7] These companies also competed for the summer commuter traffic from the Yorkshire coast into Sheffield. Encouraged by the success of the Leeds expresses, the North Eastern speeded up the Sheffield summer service via York, operated jointly with the Midland, so that from 1901 an 8.35 a.m. departure from Scarborough gave a 10.36 arrival in Sheffield, with a return at 4.42, reaching Scarborough at 6.55. The Great Central response was a train taking the slower route through Filey and Bridlington but still managing a creditable time: an 8.30am departure gave a 10.30 arrival in Sheffield, returning at 4.35 and reaching Scarborough at 7pm.

Against this background was played out the entertaining spectacle of the day excursions. A feature of the line since its opening, they must often have been a nightmare for both staff and passengers in the early days when a bevy of small engines struggled to handle an immense snake of short, four-wheeled carriages bearing anything up to a thousand passengers and likely to arrive home several hours late. By the eighteen-seventies, things were better organised and one locomotive was capable of handling six hundred passengers - typically twenty third-class carriages and a pair of guard's vans.

Excursions may be divided into two categories: public excursions running usually on Sundays, Bank Holidays and the local holidays of industrial towns in the North of England, and what would now be termed charter trains, run for parties of office and factory staff, Sunday schools and friendly societies. Two examples of the latter are drawn from consecutive days in July 1874.[8] On the fourteenth, a train was run for 800 Oddfellows from Birtley (on Tyneside) at a fare of 4 shillings (20p) third-class, leaving Birtley at 5.30 am, picking up more passengers at Durham and travelling via the Thirsk & Malton line to arrive at Scarborough at 10.15. The next day another was run from South Shields for the NER's own workmen and their families at a special fare of one shilling, departing at the apparently undaunting hour of 4.30am.

Peak congestion came at bank holidays with, for instance, 36 special trains being dealt with on the 1906 August Bank Holiday although a single firm's outing could make inordinate demands - such as the 22 special trains required on one day in 1894 to convey the employees of Bass & Co., the brewers. The problem

with excursions was that they all wanted to arrive between about 8 and 10 a.m., so the trains had to be dealt with smartly at the station and then despatched to sidings for the day; fortunately there might be a longer spread of departure times.

Prior to the opening of Londesborough Road Station, excursions had to be dealt with at platforms 1 and 2, number 3 being reserved principally for the regular York and Hull trains, while the main siding accommodation was that at Gasworks Up and Down although the two up sidings at Falsgrave could be pressed into use. Whenever possible, the company used platform 1 together with the Gasworks Down sidings; the first excursion would arrive in that platform, unload and uncouple its engine. The carriages would then be drawn off by the station pilot and taken to Gasworks Down, while the train engine despatched itself to a nearby siding. The platform was then clear for the next excursion whose empty carriages would, in theory, be taken away by the train engine off the first one, which then went to the engine shed. In practice it was often better for the Scarborough pilot engines to carry out these duties, rather than rely on drivers less familiar with the layout. On busy occasions trains were despatched to Seamer (or even further afield) and stored there, though this meant cluttering up the busy main line with empty stock workings.

The Bass excursions provide a remarkable example of this working. One was run on Friday 17 June 1898 for the employees of the Burton-on-Trent brewery, their families and a number of customers.[9] Between 3.30 and 5.50 a.m. the Midland Railway despatched 15 trains with a ten minute headway. The first was scheduled to complete its 134 mile run at 7.10 with the last reaching Scarborough at 9.30. All were to be received at Platform 1, but both excursion platforms (1 & 2) were used for the return journeys which were spread between 8.10 and 10.45 p.m., giving a last arrival at Burton at 2.45 a.m. Following the safe arrival of the last outward train at Scarborough, a telegram was despatched to Burton and a notice posted up on the brewery gates to confirm that all was well and confound the rumour-mongers who were wont to spread scare stories about railway accidents.

Bass were regular visitors to the town. Their previous excursion had been just four years earlier, on 15 June 1894. On that occasion there were 21 specials from Burton and one for their London staff.

Against all this activity, the freight and, indeed, the passenger traffic originating on the line assumed a relatively modest role, although the fish traffic warranted a daily express to London; in May 1884, for example, there was a 5.25 p.m. departure from Scarborough, supplemented by another half an hour later. One can reconstruct the picture to some extent from the monthly returns and annual statistics for stations on the line.

Table 6.1 shows the total monthly revenue from bookings at stations on the Scarborough line during 1870, covering both passenger and goods traffic but excluding all the incoming holiday and excursion business.[10] Its seasonal nature is obvious, with Summer revenue swollen by holidaymakers making local outings - not to mention fish traffic, which made up £1,732 of the September receipts. The seasons are contrasted in Table 6.2, showing the number of passengers booked at each station during the months of January and August. The picture at Scarborough is much as one might expect though it is significant that the Summer increase in first and second class passengers was proportionately much greater than that in third class. The relative importance of the wayside stations can be found by extracting the figures for Malton, Seamer and Scarborough from the total number of passengers booked during July; this leaves the others contributing only 18% of that total.

Table 6.3 illustrates the pattern of traffic at Malton from 1885 to 1914, indicating the importance of livestock traffic at this market town and the lack of scope for growth in rural passenger traffic. A warning note is struck by the rise in station expenses, from 15% of revenue in 1899 to 18% in 1905 and 24% by 1914. A similar trend is evident at Scarborough, whose passenger figures for the same period appear in Table 6.4; there the very considerable increase in expenses can be related in part to the opening of Londesborough Road Station, and the 1914 ratio of 17% seems quite modest once one remembers that the revenue quoted includes none of the incoming holiday or excursion traffic.

Scarborough's incoming coal traffic was substantial, forming the bulk of the coal, coke, lime and limestone class traffic, which was fairly steady from year to year with a prewar peak of 73,509 tons in 1914. By comparison, goods traffic was fairly modest. The town was very much a consumer of goods rather than a producer, as borne out by the figures for 1898, the peak year for goods traffic under the NER.[11] At 29,246 tons, the goods

forwarded differed little from Malton's *exports* whereas goods received amounted to 57,188 tons. The total goods station revenue was £36,349 against station expenses of £3,911. Ironically, the opening of the new Gallows Close Goods Station was followed by a rise in expenses and a fall in traffic, charted in Table 6.5. By 1914 expenses were up to £5,324 while revenue had fallen to £27,601.

The North Eastern's monopoly of the local railway network made it a natural target for criticism, and a controversy that brewed up during 1873 suggests that it was not always sensitive to this. At the beginning of that decade the NER offered fortnightly returns at cheap rates to its seaside resorts, allowing up to a two-week stay for holidaymakers who could not afford the longer break beloved of the Victorian middle class. Under pressure from a steep rise in costs, notably coal prices which more than doubled between 1870 and 1872, the company sought economies.[12] One such was the withdrawal of fortnightly returns, so that in 1873 the only comparably priced ticket available was a weekend return.

This was of great concern to the hoteliers of Scarborough, used as they were to seeing a steady rise in bednights year on year. A fall in numbers during the early summer of 1873, other than at the first class hotels, was blamed on the railway's new pricing policy, marginal as this factor may seem, and so the Town Council raised the issue with Henry Tennant, the NER General Manager.[13] They made no progress and the issue was taken up by a shareholder at the company's half-yearly meeting in August. On this occasion the Chairman, George Leeman, rubbed salt into the wound with his cavalier response that one party (in Scarborough) *fostered excursion trains, and another thought that they were the curse of the town. The Board had to judge between the two of what was best to be done.* This, of course, was pure sophistry. Then, as now, the merits of day excursion trade divided the business community but that had nothing to do with this issue.

Concern was also expressed about the inadequacy of the station to handle excursion traffic, and the town council complained of excursion passengers hanging around outside because of the lack of facilities inside. This brought a sturdy response from Tennant, hardly inclined to soothe matters, to the effect that visitors were clearly *desirous of leaving Scarborough before the time at which the trains are advertised to depart*, adding that he would *take*

A Great Northern Railway excursion train resting in the sidings at Scarborough, while the passengers enjoy the town, probably about the end of the nineteenth century. Number 723, one of Patrick Stirling's "Standard Goods" stands at the head of its train, buffered up to a NER four-wheeled brake third.
Photo: C.B. Foster collection.

A NER charabanc party waiting to leave Scarborough Station forecourt on a trip to Forge Valley.
Photo: J.F. Mallon collection.

care that this point is not lost sight of and consider whether we may not arrange for the earlier departure of the return trains.

It is not altogether surprising therefore that in 1875 an approach was made to the Midland Railway to see if they would extend their system to the town. This they declined to consider, indeed as time went on it became increasingly unlikely that any other major company would wish to promote a competing line to Scarborough. There was little to attract them in the way of lucrative freight traffic, while those which wished a share of the passenger business were already running trains over the NER. There remained the possible threat from new local ventures.

Ironically, this appeared most serious in 1883 just as the NER was engaged in spending about £23,000 to remodel the passenger station. At that time the Hull & Barnsley Railway (H & B) was under construction and a Scarborough & East Riding Railway was formed to build a new line across the Wolds to Market Weighton and a junction with the H & B at Howden. This won the backing of the Town Council but investors were less forthcoming and in March 1884 the promoters came to an accommodation with the NER. A truncated scheme, for links between existing NER lines, was opposed by a minority of promoters, who considered this to be a sellout, but got Parliamentary approval in 1885 as the grandly-titled Scarborough Bridlington & West Riding Junction Railway. In the event, only one portion was built - from Driffield to Market Weighton, where it met the North Eastern's branches from Selby and York. This opened in 1890 and was worked from the outset by the NER, who found it a useful alternative holiday route to Bridlington and Scarborough; they took it over completely in 1913.

Under George Gibb, Tennant's successor, the North Eastern not only brought its costs under control but adopted an energetic marketing strategy for its holiday resorts, aiming to develop a holiday market pitched between the excursion and the long stay. Weekend and Ten-Day tickets were offered for both first and third-class travel while there were combined railway and hotel weekend tickets available for third-class only.[14] In Scarborough, the company had two classes of hotel in its scheme: in 1899 Scale A embraced the Grand, Prince of Wales, Royal, Cambridge, Balmoral and Pavilion (just by the station) while Scale B covered the Hydropathic, Salisbury, Bell and Alexandra. Travel from York, with two nights stay and full board from dinner on the first evening to breakfast on the second morning, cost 23/-6 (117.5p) Scale A and 18/-6 (92.5p) Scale B; additional nights (Friday and/or Monday) could be had for a further 10/- (50p) and 7/-6 (37.5p) respectively.

For people staying at the resort there was an early form of rover ticket, offering unlimited travel for periods of one or two weeks. Number 4, taking in the area bounded by Scarborough, Malton and Whitby, cost £1-14-6 (172.5p) first class for a week and nineteen shillings (95p) second class. Number 5 took in Scarborough, Malton, Driffield and Bridlington and cost £1-8-6 (142.5p) first class. Other offerings included Circular Tour Tickets for people wishing to base their holiday on a number of centres.

In addition, the years leading up to the First World War saw the introduction of motor charabanc services, operating from the forecourt of Scarborough Station. Under powers obtained in its 1905 Act, the railway began operating road motor services at Scarborough in April 1906. By 1914 there were up to nine full and half-day tours daily in Summer.[15] The most ambitious of these was a 73 mile round trip to Rievaulx and Helmsley, leaving at 10.15am and returning at 6pm for a fare of 7/-6 (37.5p), while a popular half-day tour was to Forge Valley and Hackness, 18 miles for 2/-6 (12.5p).

Table 6.1 Total Monthly Revenue (including Fish Traffic) from bookings at all Scarborough Branch Stations in 1870

Note - revenue is rounded to the nearest pound

January	£2,644	February	£2,238
March	£2,598	April	£3,171
May	£3,325	June	£3,813
July	£4,738	August	£8,118
September	£9,435	October	£6,927
November	£4,253	December	£3,348

Table 6.3 Traffic at Malton: 1885-1914

Year Sampled	1885	1899	1905	1914
Passengers Booked*	103,881	113,939	100,884	97,488
Passenger Revenue(£)	10,232	11,380	11,246	11,556
Livestock Numbers	67,528	117,203	106,884	124,146
Coal, coke & lime (tons)	19,743	21,820	21,206	19,588
Goods Forwarded (tons)	18,264	27,600	24,110	23,822
Goods Received (tons)	26,140	30,331	33,324	32,142
Total Income(£)	unknown	28,918	29,354	32,804
Station Expenses(£)	3,245	4,381	5,268	7,800

* NOTE - *to form an estimate of total passenger traffic handled at Malton one should multiply the number of passengers booked at Malton Station by approximately 2.2.*

Table 6.2 Number of passengers booked at each station during January and August 1870

month	January			August		
	first	second	third	first	second	third
Haxby	13	54	210	23	79	326
Strensall	4	97	186	4	90	312
Flaxton	32	164	239	37	173	403
Barton Hill	29	122	173	60	130	268
Kirkham Abbey	30	123	99	52	124	175
Castle Howard	2	67	119	17	92	218
Huttons Ambo	21	80	163	30	115	297
Malton	348	1158	3441	499	2018	5184
Rillington	16	197	339	26	238	447
Knapton	16	53	62	26	51	120
Heslerton	18	175	197	30	133	261
Weaverthorpe	60	218	273	67	278	370
Ganton	56	207	180	43	215	283
Seamer	17	194	615	25	348	980
Scarborough	705	1326	3414	2654	5020	8585
Totals	1,367	4,235	9,710	3,593	9,104	18,229
Revenue	–	£2,193	–	–	£6,283	–

Table 6.4   **Passenger Bookings at Scarborough Station: 1885-1914**

NOTES: *The table shows the numbers of passengers booked from Scarborough for four sample years, together with the revenue from these ticket sales and the total revenue from passenger class traffic (including parcels etc.) and the passenger station working expenses. The incoming passengers booked to Scarborough were, of course, very much greater than the numbers given here.*

	1885	1899	1905	1914
Passengers booked	222,042	324,711	328,304	309,765
Passenger revenue (£)	37,525	49,031	50,520	47,979
Total Station Income (£)	unknown	58,941	57,931	56,516
Station Expenses (£)	3,314	5,866	6,441	9,728

Table 6.5   **Scarborough Goods Station Traffic: 1870 - 1954**

NOTES: *The traffic figures are for Scarborough Goods Station only and do not include coal and coke traffic or livestock. They are presented as annual averages for five-year periods, expressed as a percentage of the goods handled during 1898, a year which saw the peak goods traffic during NER ownership. The 1898 figures are:*

Goods Forwarded from Scarborough - 29,246 tons
Goods Received at Scarborough - 57,188 tons

The busiest year ever was 1926, which saw 12,861 tons forwarded and 77,180 tons received.

Period	Forwarded	Received	Period	Forwarded	Received
1870-4	30%	43%	1910-14	56%	80%
1875-9	35	64	1915-19	47	64
1880-4	33	65	1920-4	41	95
1885-9	37	58	1925-9	43	125
1890-4	55	68	1930-4	30	91
1895-9	99	87	1935-9	32	91
1900-04	90	96	1940-4	61	68
1905-09	75	86	1945-9	47	78
			1950-4	40	60

Horse parade at Gallows Close Goods Station. Photo: J. F. Mallon Collection.

Scarborough's B16 (NER Class S3) Number 845 heading past the recently-closed Kirkham Abbey Station in 1934 with the daily coal train from Gascoigne Wood. Photo: Ian C. Allen (photographer) Ken Hoole collection.

Chapter 7

The LNER Era

The North Eastern Railway entered 1914 apparently in the best of health. George Gibb and his successor as General Manager, Alexander Butterworth, had turned the tide of a rising operating ratio (ratio of expenses to receipts), traffic was buoyant and the Scarborough Line enjoyed a better service than ever before. The picture was somewhat misleading, however. Other countries were competing with the heavy industries on which the economy of the North East was based and two in particular, Germany and the USA, were proving more efficient in basic industries such as steel. The results of this were to be seen when international trade was re-established following the agony of the First World War.

For the first few months the War had little effect on services. Then, with the railways brought under Government control, their workshops diverted into munitions and young men enlisting in the Forces, services were reduced and slowed down. Luxuries like the non-stop Leeds express and through trains to Kings Cross vanished. Costs also rose sharply: wages increased and the NER's locomotive coal costs rose from an average of 61p per ton in 1914 to 99.5p by 1918.

When hostilities ended, the railways were run down and the Government unwilling to fully relinquish control. Even by 1922 services had not recovered to prewar levels, as is evident from the advertised passenger train mileage on the Scarborough line. Comparing timetables for July 1914 and 1922, the weekday mileage was down from 2047 to 1593, a reduction of 22.1%, while the Sunday service had dropped from 337 to 214, a fall of 36.4%.[1] Winter schedules showed even more dramatic falls of 32.8%, from 1265 to 849, on weekdays and 50%, from 168 to 84, on Sundays.

Recovery was in hand, however. The Leeds non-stop express was reinstated and the through service to Kings Cross, while from 19 July 1922 the company showed some innovation in its local services with the introduction of a *Rail Motor Bus* between Strensall and York, some workings being extended through to Copmanthorpe on the Leeds line. Meanwhile the company's senior officers were preoccupied with the Grouping which took effect from the end of the year. The North Eastern came into the LNER as the largest and most profitable partner, yet from 1922 the heavy engineering industries which provided its wealth were in decline, with falling exports. Although the Depression which paralysed the world's great economies did not arrive until 1929, the North East was in recession long before this and the LNER had to be cautious about its investment programmes from the outset.

The main problem the LNER faced was no longer the traditional stimulus of competition with other railways but how to come to terms with road transport. At this stage the private car was not a serious challenge, relatively few people could afford one and mass ownership was not envisaged, instead their concern lay with bus services and lorries. They fought back in three ways: improving their own services and marketing, investing in road services as feeders to the railway and substituting these for passenger trains in a few cases. Although the NER had operated some road services prior to the War, the railways' legal powers in this respect were unclear and open to challenge so all four main-line companies obtained Parliamentary powers in 1928 to own and operate road transport.

The LNER used these to invest in established operators, such as United Automobile Services and the West Yorkshire Road Car Company, and on 26 June 1930 the company's Traffic Committee agreed to withdraw passenger services from a number of rural routes, including the local service on the Scarborough line.[2] This made good sense; most of the wayside stations were located well away from the villages they served and the company was able to offer a better service, connecting with trains at York, Malton and Scarborough, through the United and West Yorkshire buses.

Table 7.1 gives statistics for passengers booked at the Scarborough Branch stations from 1902 to 1926.[3] This does not show the full extent of traffic, which requires details of

FIRST CLASS CLUB SALOON

No. 2/1240. BUILT YORK 1899 CONVERTED OCT. 1922

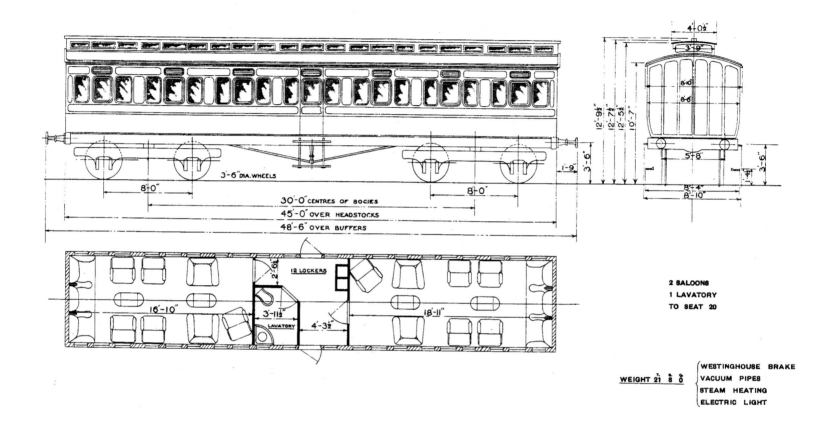

The Scarborough-Leeds Club Saloon, from an official NER Diagram. J. F. Addyman collection.

tickets collected and season tickets, and would typically be about 2.2 times greater (except at Scarborough itself, where the disparity is much larger). These figures nonetheless clearly show the trend in business.

For most stations the War brought a modest fall in passengers, although Strensall received a massive boost due to infantry training on Strensall Common. The brief postwar recovery is reflected in the figures for 1920 but then road competition started to bite, particularly at Strensall and Haxby where buses were creaming off the most lucrative traffic. The railmotor brought a brief respite, seen in the 1923 bookings, but the decline resumed and bookings at these two stations fell by 48% from 1923 to 1926.

From 22 September 1930, passenger services were withdrawn from all the intermediate stations except Malton and Seamer. It is easy now to argue that the LNER did not go far enough and that the same treatment should have been handed out to routes such as the Forge Valley line from Pickering to Seamer which, inexplicably, retained its passenger service until 1950. Another batch of closures was agreed by the Traffic Committee on 27 November, as a result of which the Ryedale line from Malton to Gilling lost its passenger service at the end of the year although remaining open for freight and holiday trains.

The withdrawal of regular passenger services did not mean the total closure of the wayside stations on the Scarborough line, which retained their platforms for excursion use and continued to handle coal and goods traffic. In addition, special arrangements were made for some forms of traffic formerly carried by passenger train, such as parcels, and a small number of passengers continued to be booked on the parcels trains although this was not an advertised facility. The forecast savings are presented in Table 7.2, where it can be seen that by far the dominant cost lay in the locomotive department. Economies were also achieved by downgrading a number of station signalboxes, such as Haxby, from block posts to gate boxes, staffed by the lower-paid grade of porter-signalman. In such cases, the block was only switched back in when working the station sidings or when the heavy Summer traffic required a reduction in the length of the block sections.

While weeding out business for which the railway was no longer well suited, the LNER continued to develop the holiday traffic with considerable success, aided by a highly effective publicity department. In Summer 1927 an additional express train was introduced between Kings Cross and Scarborough, the *Scarborough Flier* (later changed to *Flyer*). Leaving London at 11.50 a.m. it was scheduled to reach Scarborough at 4.18 p.m., with one stop at York, while the up train left Scarborough at 3.30 p.m. With Gresley's new Pacific (4-6-2) locomotives working the train between London and York, running times were progressively reduced until from July 1935 the schedule for the 230 miles became 235 minutes (ten minutes longer on Saturdays), without an advertised stop at York. This compares with 289 minutes for the pre-war luncheon-car express. The Pacifics did not work through to Scarborough, the turntables being too small for them, and so the train in fact stopped to change engines on either the centre roads at York Station or the goods lines to its south.

The Leeds service progressed in a mixed fashion though the initial developments were promising enough. Having reinstated the non-stop express, the NER further responded to demand by introducing a first-class club saloon, for which a committee of passengers guaranteed a supplementary payment. The vehicle concerned had a curious history; built in 1899 it had been altered for wartime use in the special train of the Director General of Tranportation, Sir Eric Geddes, formerly Deputy General Manager of the NER and, from 1919, first Minister of Transport. It was converted for use on the Leeds-Scarborough service in October 1922.

Despite this provision patronage must have declined, for the non-stop business express was finally abolished at the end of the 1929 Summer season, the club saloon being despatched to the Scarborough-Hull service, where the concept had originated. For the commuter, the comparable journey in the 1934 timetable entailed an 8.10 a.m. departure from Scarborough to reach Leeds at 9.37, with a return at 4.42, getting back to Scarborough at 6.10. Excluding the *Scarborough Flier*, the best expresses now covered York-Scarborough in 55 minutes. There was, however, a Summer Saturdays Only non-stop holiday express between Leeds and Scarborough, leaving Leeds at

10.10 a.m. and Scarborough at 2 p.m., and conveying a through carriage to Bradford.

Government Aid to depressed areas enabled the LNER to embark on a new coaching stock construction programme which led to the displacement of NER carriages from the Leeds service. The company planned to introduce five new eight-car sets from May 1936.[4] It is unclear whether the plan kept to schedule or was deferred to September 1937 when buffet cars were introduced.

Developments in coaching stock were one factor in the disappearance of a typically North Eastern feature, the ticket platform. In the days when most trains were operated by stock without communicating vestibules between carriages, ticket inspection was a problem. Most of the NER's larger stations were *open* and tickets were not collected at the platform barriers. In the absence of through corridors they could not be inspected en route and so ticket platforms, very narrow wooden platforms, were placed by the tracks at the approaches to the main stations. Trains stopped there briefly while a small group of highly agile ticket collectors leaped from one compartment to the next. At York, express trains coming off the Scarborough line were dealt with at a platform perched on the embankment near Queen Anne's Lane, while tickets on the stopping trains were collected at Haxby. Prior to the opening of Londesborough Road Station, Scarborough had a ticket platform on the up side approaching Falsgrave Box and this was replaced by one at Seamer. Malton also had one, originally installed at the end of 1859.

The spread of vestibuled corridor stock, and the introduction of open saloon carriages for excursion traffic, meant one could employ travelling ticket collectors on an increasing number of trains but the LNER's solution was to introduce ticket barriers at York and Scarborough.

1932 saw a drastic slump in business throughout the LNER system, but the following years brought an encouraging growth in holiday passenger traffic at Scarborough, aided by the provision of more Sunday services and such innovations as *Penny a Mile* holiday returns (fares based on the single journey mileage) and the Observation Circular Tour introduced in 1933 from Scarborough to Whitby via Pickering and returning by the coast. Passenger arrivals grew from just over 550,000 in 1932 to 685,627 in 1933 and 739,654 the following year.[5] These figures were based on tickets actually collected and did not include passengers travelling on holiday season tickets, estimated to be about 125,000 in 1934. The heavy traffic on Summer Saturdays, the changeover day for holidaymakers staying in the resort, meant the duplication of many scheduled trains, including the *Scarborough Flier,* with corresponding pressure on the inconvenient layout of Scarborough Central.

An early move to improve operation was the introduction of a local *Control*, based at Falsgrave Signalbox and linked by telephone to the other boxes between Seamer Junction and Scarborough as well as the yardmasters at Gasworks and Gallows Close Sidings.[6] Beginning with the 1924 season, it brought immediate benefits: Control was able to reschedule movements to cope with out-of-course running, a frequent experience, and provided for the first time a single focus from which information could be got as to train running and the whereabouts of empty stock.

The Scarborough Control was a summer weekend and bank holiday job for one of the staff of York District Control. There were also seasonal posts for foremen and operating staff drawn from other stations, while a summer spent helping the stationmaster provided valuable experience for traffic apprentices, working their way up the management ladder. Table 7.3 shows the pattern of train arrivals and disposal for the August Bank Holiday Sunday of a later period, 1956, based on the station operating schedule drawn up by one such assistant, Ken Appleby, who later became Area Manager, York.[7] Based on forecast train lengths, the schedule showed the platforms and carriage sidings to be used but the Seamer signalman was expected to assess the composition of each train as it passed and report this to Control, so that the platforms could be reallocated if necessary. Control would contact the yardmasters before despatching empty stock to the sidings, its location was then recorded on boards at the back of Falsgrave box, together with the availability of train crews.

As well as the inevitable complications caused by trains running out of course, York Control could put a spanner in the works by announcing that, due to passenger numbers, trains had been unexpectedly duplicated and Scarborough must fit in an extra one, with at best an hour's warning. To do so entailed close cooperation between Falsgrave Control and the stationmaster, while at busy times a locomotive inspector was despatched from York to sort out the work of the train crews.

For many years serious difficulties were caused by the Whitby trains, which used the short bays on the south side of the station and had both to cross the main lines and reverse to get to and from Falsgrave Tunnel. Coming into Scarborough, for instance, the train stood on the line serving Londesborough Road Station while its engine ran round and then drew it across to the opposite side of the station. By 1933 the problem had become extreme and then, with apparent simplicity, a solution was found. Platform 1 was extended and a separate bay, Platform 1A, was formed at its west end for the sole use of the Whitby trains and able to take an engine and five carriages. Engines were allowed to propel (i.e. push) their trains into the new platform and so the conflicting movements were removed. It was completed in time for the 1934 season and the stationmaster reported that *but for the relief provided by the new 1A platform we should have been up against an almost insuperable task, in relation to our maintaining anything approaching scheduled times at the peak period.*[8] The loss of part of the west end of platform 1 due to this work was compensated by extending it into the cabstand area at the opposite end. Since the new platform was a very long way from the station entrance, Whitby train departures were made 3 minutes later than the advertised time

Despite these changes, Scarborough Central still had only three platforms capable of handling long trains. The sort of problems this led to are exemplified by the summer holiday trains from Glasgow; even in the nineteen-fifties the return train had to be marshalled in two parts, in platforms 8 and 9, and then one portion was drawn out and backed onto the other, blocking the approach to the other short bays in the process. A scheme had been devised in 1925 to rationalise the station layout, abolishing platforms 1 and 2 to make room for the tracks from six new platforms of uniform length, two within each section of the trainshed, served by traversers at the buffer stops so as to facilitate the release of train engines.[9] The LNER could not afford to do this at the time but the proposal was kept in reserve, though in the end

nothing happened. Meanwhile they set about tidying up the booking facilities in such a way as to reduce the numbers of staff needed. A catalyst for station improvements was the £7,500 received from Scarborough Corporation in 1931 as compensation in connection with the widening of Valley Bridge Road, which impinged on the coalyard.[10]

Another source of income was the exploitation of underused parts of the station site. Following the opening of Londesborough Road Station, the excursion waiting rooms and booking office adjoining platform 1 had been converted into a parcels office, and the cab road which served them had fallen out of general passenger use. In September 1933 the LNER agreed to lease to H. A. Whitaker & Company a site for motor vehicle showrooms and workshops.[11] The *Station Garage* became established with a frontage onto Westborough and extending back to bridge over the former excursion cab road. This brought in £300 p.a., a sum more than doubled by extensions onto other spare corners of the station during the following three years.

Motor vehicles were playing an increasing role in the LNER's own business, notably in the replacement of horses for local cartage. The two came together at Malton, where the company had a significant traffic in racehorses for the local training stables, the horseboxes being conveyed by passenger trains on which the NER had forwarded 1,618 horses from Malton in 1908 and received 1,238. In response to road competition the LNER purchased two *Road Motor Horse Boxes* for trials and in November 1931 agreed to add a further two.[12] These were not used simply for local travel to and from railheads but often for the full journey to the racecourse where they could do it more speedily than a railway vehicle which had to be transferred between trains. In 1934 stabling for the motor horseboxes was sought in the disused power station of the North Eastern Electric Supply Company, just across the road from Malton Station.

Thanks to railway lobbying, commercial road traffic was governed by a stringent licensing system and the Malton horse traffic illustrates the ruthless way in which the LNER was able to use this to stifle competition. In July 1934, Peter Kelly of Malton bought a four-stall motor horsebox for £1,150 and set up in rivalry with the LNER who thereby lost a good deal of traffic.[13] The company appealed against his being granted a carrier's licence and, although the Traffic Commissioners gave him one, this decision was overturned by an Appeal Tribunal in February 1935. Having thus put Mr. Kelly out of business, the LNER were concerned that they might forfeit the goodwill of the Malton trainers and so agreed to buy his vehicle for £1,000 and temporarily engage him to operate it.

Not all competition could be dealt with so readily and the company had to reach an accommodation with road operation. Motor lorries made huge inroads into the freight business, particularly short-haul traffic. Increasingly, freight became focused on a few railheads, notably Malton and Scarborough, where Gallows Close goods traffic peaked in 1926. The railway had to provide adequate warehousing facilities if it was to retain the business. To start off with these consisted of old goods van bodies but were replaced or supplemented by prefabricated concrete railhead stores.[14] An example of this development is provided by Silcocks (now BOCM Silcock), who entrained livestock feeds to Malton and Scarborough where the railway provided the road distribution service to farmers, an arrangement which lasted until January 1965.

The run-up to the Second World War saw the Scarborough line continuing to do well in many areas of business, though the railway enjoyed nothing like its former monopoly and the recovery in passenger numbers was not matched by a commensurate increase in revenue, due to fare cuts. While the war years brought a serious disruption of normal activity, there were more passengers, though many were now on military business; almost a quarter of those handled at Scarborough during the first half of 1943 were working on RAF airfields. This brought more business during the winter months without much change in the summer figures.

Even in the middle of the conflict the LNER was making plans for postwar development. These included the reconstruction of Scarborough Station but this was a lower priority than the provision of a station for a new form of holiday centre, the *Butlin's* holiday camp at Filey.[15] The largest holiday camp in Britain at the time, it was begun before the war but on completion in 1940 was requisitioned by the Air Ministry. It finally opened to holidaymakers in 1945 and, with a potential of 8,000 visitors per week, was an important customer for the LNER which constructed a branch to it during 1946.[16] It proved a very successful investment, handling holiday trains from as far afield as Glasgow. More modestly, Gallows Close was the venue for the LNER's first installation of an electric conveyor to ease the handling of sundries, this being brought into use in November 1946.

Before much else could be achieved, however, the LNER had ceased to exist, swept under the British Transport Commission by the Attlee Government's nationalisation scheme, which took effect from 1 January 1948.

Table 7.1   Developments in Passenger Traffic at Intermediate Stations 1900-1934

	1 1902 1914	2 1915 1919	3 1920	4 1921	5 1922	6 1923	7 1924	8 1925	9 1926	10 1934
Haxby	21080	106	104	82	81	105	77	77	55	498
Strensall	30017*	260	87	79	70	83	52	46	43	4155
Flaxton	13502	86	138	81	77	75	72	70	60	223
Barton Hill	7951	84	94	87	82	77	71	70	48	154
Kirkham Abbey	5863	99	103	96	95	85	81	71	?	62
Castle Howard	6780	91	112	99	94	86	90	83	67	410
Huttons Ambo	8994	90	101	85	77	69	66	66	55	182
Malton	102107	84	108	93	90	88	92	91	70	36582
Rillington	13531	92	100	81	81	78	78	77	54	257
Knapton	4680	84	77	68	64	62	66	53	42	101
Heslerton	6535	82	96	78	77	65	62	53	34	28
Sherburn	10667	87	114	89	79	68	55	49	36	329
Ganton	9273	100	125	110	98	85	64	65	49	102
Seamer	27195	95	108	76	77	78	71	71	54	4815
Scarborough	319995	76	120	106	87	94	86	86	73	155085

NOTES:
Column 1 is the average number of passengers booked annually at each station during the period 1902-1914
Column 2 is the annual average for the period 1915-1919 expressed as a percentage of the figure in column 1.
Columns 3 to 9 are the annual figures expressed as a percentage of column 1.
Column 10 is the actual number of passengers booked in 1934. At closed stations they were travelling by the parcels train and, possibly, excursions.
* this average for Strensall excludes 1914, because of the distorting effect of the abnormally high number of bookings that year: 62,508, due to the War.

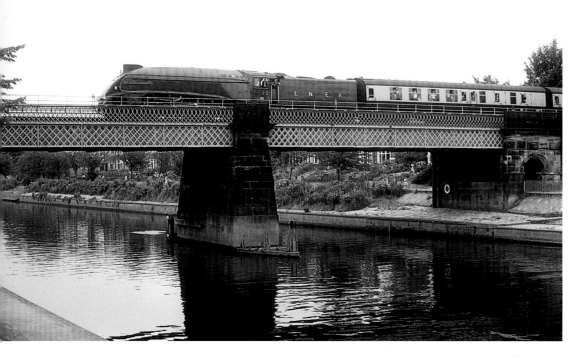

Scarborough Railway Bridge, York, with A4 Pacific Number 4498 "Sir Nigel Gresley" hauling the Scarborough Spa Express in August 1981
Photo: J. F. Addyman.

Stanier Pacific, "Duchess of Hamilton," crossing the Derwent at Low Hutton on August Bank Holiday Sunday 1994
Photo: Bill Fawcett.

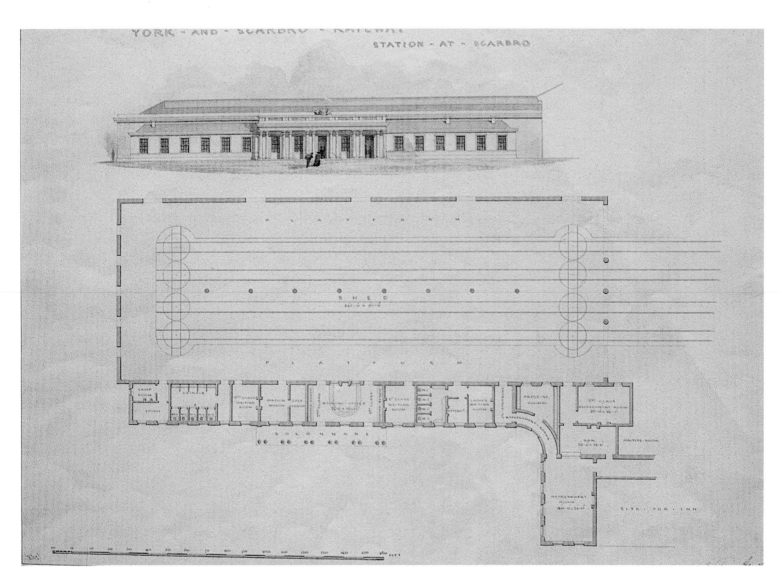

G.T. Andrews' original design for Scarborough Station, from a drawing in the Victoria & Albert Museum. Photo: Bill Fawcett.

Table 7.2   Balance Sheet for the Withdrawal of Stopping Trains from the Scarborough Line

Annual Savings: . . . . £
   Locomotive Power 4,512
   Carriages 903
   Station Staff 1,628
   Station Stores 85
   Lighting and Fuel 60
   Station Repairs and Painting 100

Estimated Gross Saving 7,288

Estimated Loss of Revenue 3,669

Net Annual Saving 3,619

Table 7.3   Bank Holiday Working Arrangements at Scarborough

Key: TN *Train Number.* Pf *Platform.* LR *Londesborough Road.*
Carriage Stabling: Rem *Remain in Platform,* To 6 *To Platform 6,* GD *Gasworks Down,* GU *Gasworks Up,* GC *Gallows Close,* F *Falsgrave,* W *Washbeck Yard.*

ARRIVALS AT SCARBOROUGH CENTRAL AND LONDESBOROUGH ROAD

TN	Due	Pf	From	Stabling	Forms
324	05.32	1	York	Rem	08.28 to Manchester Victoria
318	09.46	2	York	Rem	10.20 to Hull
341	09.56	1	Leeds	To 8/9	17.55 to York
215	10.06	1	York	GD	20.10 from Platform 1 to York
752	10.16	1	Knottingley	GD	18.50 from 2 to Knottingley
600	10.21	5	Hull	To 6/7	20.44 to Hull
753	10.35	1	Knottingley	GD	19.20 from 2 to Knottingley
322	10.45	3	York	To 4	19.00 to Leeds
346	10.55	2	Bradford	GD	20.20 from 2 to Bradford
211	11.05	LR1	Castleford	W	20.50 from 2 to Castleford
323	11.26	2	York	GU	19.10 from 1 to York
10	11.26	1A	Bishop Auckland	GD	18.33 from 1A to Bishop
53	11.40	1A	Darlington	GD	20.03 from 1A to Stockton
750	11.45	LR1	Wakefield	GC	22.10 from LR 1 to Wakefield
214	11.55	LR2	Harrogate	Rem	18.15 to Harrogate

TN	Due	Pf	From	Stabling	Forms	
11	11.56	1A	Middlesbrough	GD	18.44	from 1A to Middlesbro'
601	12.00	5	Hull	Rem	18.05	to Hull
324	12.06	3	York	Rem	14.10	to Leeds
97	12.16	2	Newcastle	F	22.20	from 4 to Newcastle
50	12.20	1A	West Hartlepool	GD	19.03	from 1A to West H'pool
262	12.30	LR1	Leeds	GC	21.20	from LR 1 to Leeds
263	12.40	LR1	Leeds	GC	21.30	from LR 1 to Leeds
364	12.50	1	Ackworth	GU	18.38	from 1 to Ackworth
52	12.56	1A	Middlesbrough	GD	18.03	from 1A to Middlesbro'
365	13.08	LR1	Bolton on Dearne	GC	21.00	from LR 1 to Bolton/D
47	13.16	1A	Stockton	GD	17.33	from 1A to Stockton
266	13.18	1	Kippax	GU	21.10	from 1 to Kippax
372	13.30	LR1	Nottingham	GC	20.38	from LR 1 to Nottingham
13	13.33	1A	Middlesbrough	GD	18.18	from 1A to Middlesbro'
281	13.36	LR1	Hull	GC	19.33	from LR 1 to Hull
876	13.50	1	Bradford	GD	22.00	from 2 to Bradford
54	13.51	1A	Middlesbrough	Rem	14.25	to Whitby
91	14.02	LR1	Newcastle	GC	22.40	from LR 2 to Newcastle
326	14.11	2	York	F	19.27	from 9 to York
362	14.22	1	Laisterdyke	GD	22.30	from 3 to Laisterdyke
885	14.32	LR1	Chesterfield	GC	22.50	from LR 1 to Chesterf'd
92	14.42	LR1	Hebburn	GC	21.40	from LR 2 to Hebburn
888	14.52	1	Rotherham	GD	23.20	from 2 to Rotherham
887	15.02	2	Heeley	GD	23.00	from 1 to Heeley
890	15.12	1	Burton on Trent	GC	23.10	from 3 to Burton
46	15.24	1A	Middlesbrough	GD	19.33	from 1A to Darlington
283	16.04	3	Whitby Scenic	F	20.01	from 4 Hull Scenic
-	16.52	1A	Whitby	Rem	17.00	to Middlesbro'
325	18.01	3	York	Rem	19.55	to York
315	19.24	5	Hull	Rem	20.30	to York
-	20.59	1A	Whitby	Rem	09.18	following day to Whitby
324	21.51	1	York	GU		Spare Coaching Stock

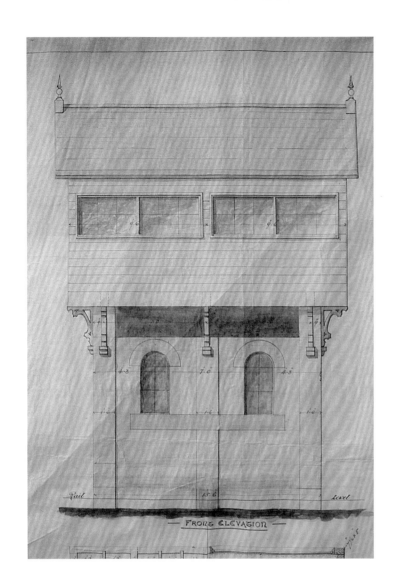

Design for Scarborough (station) Signalbox, later replaced, probably in 1899. Drawing: Ken Hoole collection.

A "Sprinter" heading past Kirkham Abbey en route from Manchester to Scarborough.
Photo: Bill Fawcett.

A "Sprinter" heading for Scarborough across the river Ouse at York.
Photo: Bill Fawcett.

Two excursions about to set off home from Londesborough Road Station in the nineteen-fifties. Framed by the characteristic McKenzie & Holland signal gantry is B16 (NER Class S3) Number 61415. On the right is a British Railways Standard Class 3MT, Number 82028. Photo: Ken Hoole.

Chapter 8

British Railways

Nationalisation saw the Scarborough line back in the NER, although this time it was the North Eastern Region of British Railways. During its first decade the new regime seemed to retain a view of the role of the railway little different from that of the LNER twenty years earlier, and a time traveller from 1905 revisiting the line fifty years later would have found little altered except for the locomotives and carriages. Even the wayside stations, long closed to passengers, had changed little in appearance though reduced to coal traffic and a dwindling portion of freight.

The B.R. Modernisation Plan, which emerged in 1955, was concerned more with technical developments than any basic change in either the role or operation of railways but a serious decline in their share of freight traffic, exacerbated by a slump in heavy engineering exports after 1957, drew the Macmillan government to a reassessment which led to the appointment of Richard Beeching as Chairman in 1961. After the publication of the Beeching Report, *The Reshaping of British Railways*, in 1963 events moved rapidly to transform both the role and shape of the system.

The first decade of British Railways saw the regions go different ways in their motive power policies, the North Eastern showing a particular interest in the utility of diesel multiple units (dmu's) on branch-line services. Developments in the high-speed diesel engine opened the way to lightweight trains with a much better power/weight ratio than steam trains and a better reliability than pre-war diesel railcars. The first NER dmu scheme was introduced between Bradford, Leeds, Harrogate and Knaresborough in June 1954 and in 4 years receipts rose 400% compared with the last year of steam operation, passengers being attracted by an improved timetable and the trains themselves, whose saloon interior with low-backed, bus-type seats gave much better all-round views than the old compartment stock.[1]

The Scarborough line continued to be steam operated but by 1957 it was expected that the Leeds-Scarborough trains would be handed over to dmu's by the end of the following year. In the event this did not happen until 7 March 1960, while steam locomotives continued to be seen on freight and excursion trains until 1967; Scarborough shed had closed on 20 May 1963 but facilities for steam engines had continued to be available in the shed yard. While the survival of steam was a boon to enthusiasts, this was a mixed blessing. Indifferent coal and declining maintenance standards brought problems not usually evident to travellers on the East Coast Main Line but all too obvious to passengers in delayed excursions, hauled by *spare* engines or goods locomotives called on to perform heroic deeds, such as the 4F 0-6-0's from Burnley's Rose Grove shed, regularly seen on excursions from East Lancashire.

A move which later had a bearing on the fortunes of the Scarborough line was the dieselisation of trans-Pennine services in January 1961. A new, regular interval timetable was introduced for the trains from Newcastle and Hull to Liverpool and Manchester. The former were operated by 2000hp, Type 4 diesel locomotives, somewhat underpowered for their task. The Hull trains received an improved type of diesel multiple unit, *Transpennine* stock with a higher than usual proportion of powered cars and standards of comfort closer to those of an express train than to the average dmu; they were, however, hampered by having the same top speed as other dmu's: 70 mph.[2]

Diesel traction barely lifted the Scarborough line schedules back to pre-war levels. Taking the Winter 1963-4 timetable as an example, the fastest time was now marginally improved to 53 minutes but that old indicator, the onetime Leeds commuter train, now required a departure at 8.02, eight minutes earlier, to achieve its pre-war arrival time of 9.37 at Leeds.

Meanwhile the *Scarborough Flyer* was heading towards an ignominious fate. Though reintroduced with a flourish of publicity in June 1950, it never regained its previous status. After the first season it ran from London on Summer Fridays and Saturdays and from Scarborough on Saturdays and Sundays. The schedule was far removed from the 235 minutes of 1935, the best being the 268 minute timing of the down trains in 1951 and 1952. Between London and York the run was split between two locomotives, changing at Grantham and usually Pacifics, but from York to Scarborough there was a risk of being hauled by anything the shedmaster had on hand, including an 0-6-0 freight engine.

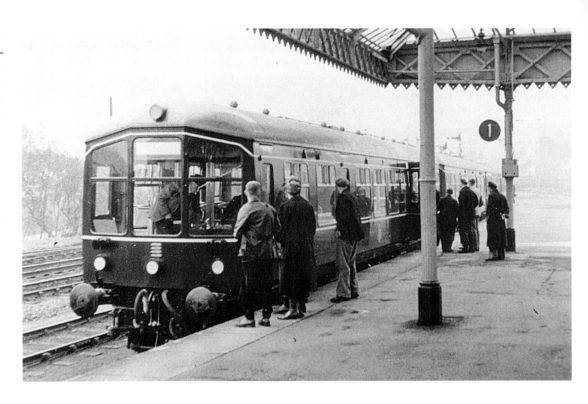

Scarborough's first sight of a British Railways diesel multiple unit. Cars - numbers 79151, 79401 and 79509 at Londesborough Road on 3 November 1955. Note the fully-glazed station roof. Photo: Ken Hoole.

A typical train of the sixties and seventies. Happy holidaymakers returning to Leeds on a Sunday evening in May 1978. The train, made up of two 4-car sets, has just left Seamer. Photo: C. B. Foster.

With a relatively leisurely schedule, most locomotives were perfectly capable of maintaining time and indeed improving on it but on busy Summer Saturdays the Flyer became prone to delay. After a time it had no regular set of coaches and latterly it was made up of any available stock, regardless of condition, thus its eventual withdrawal came as no surprise.

Throughout the nineteen-fifties passenger traffic on the line remained healthy, indeed 1959 saw over a million passengers at Scarborough, with the Whit Bank Holiday excursion stock stabled as far back up the line as Barton Hill and Strensall. Goods traffic, however, was already in decline as seen in table 6.5. Road haulage was providing flexible and cheap competition, assisted by industrial disputes on the railway.

The wayside stations had lost most of their sundries traffic to the railway's own road services, based on York, Malton and Scarborough, but continued to handle coal and local specialities, such as sugar beet for the factory at York. They were served by a pickup goods, marshalled in the sidings at Gallows Close and operating up the line to York. This and other goods services during the early fifties are detailed in Table 8.1, revealing a traditional pattern with the fastest schedule being the express goods which left Scarborough Central at 6.40 p.m. after picking up any fish wagons.

All this changed after Richard Beeching produced his report in 1963. The more hopeless branch lines had already been abandoned: the Forge Valley from Seamer Junction as far as Thornton Dale in 1950 and the Malton & Driffield, only kept going by stone traffic from Burdale, in 1958. Now, what had seemed core business was called into question. Adverse trends were already apparent in the holiday business: over the whole system the July peak, expressed as a percentage of the average traffic from October to May, had fallen from 196% (i.e. 96% above the average) in 1951 to 147% by 1961.[3] Beeching attributed this to the growth in family car ownership, though that was still at an early stage and the railway continued to handle high levels of Bank Holiday weekend traffic. Coach services also played a part while, lurking unforeseen round the corner, was the explosion in the air-charter business which was to lure so many Britons to holidays abroad and devastate many a seaside resort at home.

Holiday traffic required investment in coaching stock and locomotives which were underused for most of the year and, given the evidence of decline, Beeching favoured a move out of this area. Coupled with the abandonment of stopping-train services, other than in some suburban areas, and either the concentration or abandonment of the freight sundries business this presaged an uncertain future for the railways of Scarborough. Reaction to the Beeching Plan focused principally on the proposed branch closures, the relevant ones in this case being all the routes to Whitby, including the line from Rillington. The coastal service from Scarborough to Hull was scheduled for *modification,* a euphemism for the closure of several stations and a reduction in services.

The proposals were welcomed by the Government which had commissioned them but the following year they were out of office and the Wilson Government took a different view of transport policy, leading to the introduction of grant aid for socially desirable but uneconomic passenger services. Beeching left in 1965 but many of his proposals were implemented. One of the Whitby lines was retained, the Esk Valley route to Middlesbrough, while the Scarborough-Hull line kept its stations but the railway largely moved out of the excursion business and drastically rationalised its freight operations. The latter became a political football between successive Labour and Conservative Governments with unfortunate consequences.

The first effects of the Beeching Report were felt on the Scarborough line in 1964, with the closure of the wayside stations to goods traffic on 10 August, thirtyfour years after the withdrawal of passenger services. Just two retained goods sidings in connection with local industries: Weaverthorpe (the former Sherburn Station), on account of the construction firm - Wards of Sherburn, and Knapton, which had a private siding serving Associated British Maltsters. The Malton-Pilmoor line was also abandoned, forcing holiday trains from Scotland and Tyneside to pass through York Station; they were not even permitted to use the York goods lines as an avoiding route because of supposed signalling inadequacies.

The passenger service between Malton and Whitby was withdrawn on 8 March 1965 but Pickering remained open to goods until July of the following year, the line being maintained as far as Hargreaves' quarry at New Bridge. The route between Rillington and Pickering was then completely abandoned but the

North Riding County Council had the foresight to purchase the trackbed from Pickering to Grosmont, which reopened as the North Yorkshire Moors Railway.

The 1968 Transport Act set out a framework for railway freight, with the removal of the unprofitable sundries business to the then publicly owned National Freight Corporation (NFC) and a concentration on wagonload and trainload traffic, but the outlook was already worse than Beeching had envisaged. Household coal consumption had long been declining, with the move to electricity and gas for heating, but the exploitation of natural gas from under the North Sea brought an end to gasmaking from coal during the nineteen-sixties. 1970 saw the demolition of the production plant at Scarborough Gasworks, symbolising the loss of the most important element in the line's freight business.

The siding at Knapton was formally closed in October 1979 and Weaverthorpe in August 1981. Malton, having lost its goods shed in a fire in 1956, was eventually downgraded to a public delivery siding which closed on 3 September 1984. The transfer of sundries traffic to National Carriers (a subsidiary of the NFC) meant that Gallows Close goods station became for a time a centre for road traffic. The withdrawal of single wagon load coal deliveries saw the remaining coal traffic transferred to road, and by the Summer of 1986 all tracks had been removed from the Gallows Close site, which is now a supermarket. Latterly the only freight facility left in Scarborough was a siding for Appleton Associates oil depot, and this has now closed.

This period also saw the end of the Scarborough mail train, which made its last journey on Saturday 10 May 1980. This led to one modest economy: the signalboxes could now open later, those between Haxby Road and Barton Hill, for instance, having their opening put back from 4.20 to 6 a.m.

If the freight picture is a rather dismal reflection of happenings elsewhere on British Rail, the passenger services have improved considerably. On 14 May 1979, a regular interval service was introduced between York and Scarborough with an hourly service through most of the day. The most important development, however, was the recasting of the transpennine trains so that they ran from Scarborough, rather than Hull, to Manchester and Liverpool, thereby providing a more frequent express service from York to the west. By 1985 these were maintaining a 53 minute schedule between Scarborough and York and 153 minutes for the 112 miles (179km) between Scarborough and Manchester. Our Leeds commuter, had one still existed, would not have been too happy though, requiring a 7.45 departure and a change of trains in York to reach Leeds at 9.15, since there was no through train until 9.55.

With the dmu's at the end of their serviceable life, the transpennine service had reverted to locomotive haulage but in 1988 new *Sprinter* trains were introduced onto the line. The timings are now a little faster: York-Scarborough is done in typically 46 minutes up and 47 minutes down, while Scarborough-Manchester takes typically 143 minutes. The service, however, is enormously improved with the first train from Scarborough at 6.38 a.m. and departures at roughly hourly intervals until 8.45 p.m. A notable development was the opening in May 1993 of a line to Manchester Airport which was for a year the terminus for Scarborough trains. The winter 1994/5 timetable saw them routed instead alternately to Blackpool and Liverpool, the Hull - Manchester service having been restored several years ago. Sundays now enjoy a regular interval service, hourly in summer and two-hourly in winter. As for our Leeds commuter: a 7.29 departure now brings one to Leeds at 8.47, not quite so fast as the North Eastern's express but fitting in stops at Seamer, Malton and York.

What of the holiday traffic? Beeching's forecasts have been fulfilled, though this was largely inevitable once the railway adopted his policy of discouraging excursion and holiday relief trains. After 1964 these were steadily run down, although until recently a link with the past was maintained by *holidaymaker* services from Glasgow, operated by high-speed trains. What remains of this business is now handled by the much-enhanced regular train service. The day visitors flood in by car and at Bank Holidays the highlight can be a leisurely exploration of the A64, which handles about 30,000 vehicles on peak days. The excursion business is almost exclusively the province of coaches, which also capture much of the other holiday business with package tours.

The boom in overseas holidays caused much heartache for British resorts but Scarborough fought back, developing its conference business, and in 1981 completed a £6 million restoration and improvement of the Spa Buildings. To complement this, regular steam trains were reintroduced to the line in the form of the *Scarborough Spa Express*. This was a joint venture between British Rail, Scarborough District Council and the National Railway Museum, which provided locomotives from the national collection. Scarborough contributed £35,000 towards the restoration of the most famous of these, Gresley's streamlined Pacific *Mallard,* and also paid half the cost of reinstating a turntable in the derelict turntable pit at the site of the shed yard. Prior to this the occasional steam engine visiting Scarborough on a special had turned on the triangle at Filey Holiday Camp Station. This, however, closed in 1977. A 70 feet turntable was provided in the 60 feet pit, by extending the decking at either end, and it was tested on 18 May 1981 by the Stanier Pacific *Duchess of Hamilton* which made the first run of the Scarborough Spa Express five days later, to coincide with the reopening of the Spa Buildings.

Despite both York and Scarborough being holiday centres, the new venture did not take off to the extent expected. York, in particular, suffers from too many of its visitors making overnight stays in the course of package tours so there are not all that many long-stay tourists to explore the delights of the area. Once the novelty wore off there was insufficient traffic to sustain the Scarborough Spa Express as a commercial venture and it was gradually phased out, running for the last time in 1988. Although there still appears to be some potential for such a service, steam *specials* are few and far between, the most notable recent one being the return of *Duchess of Hamilton* on the 1994 August Bank Holiday Sunday, sponsored by its own supporters' club.

With the decline in passengers and loss of freight, the finances of the Scarborough line plunged heavily into the red, in common with most British Rail services. By January 1973, the annual loss was estimated at £543,000 and, despite subsidy, it was clearly necessary to achieve major operating economies, particularly reductions in staffing. Some of this came naturally with the abandonment of freight, unmanned operation of Seamer Station and enormous staff losses at Malton and Scarborough. Another important area of economy is the signalling department.

A costly legacy of George Hudson is the plethora of level crossings along the line; some have been replaced in the course of road improvements but the majority remain. The North Eastern Region made a number of technical innovations designed to ease their operation, notably the use of tow-motors so that the heavy wooden gates could be operated electrically.

The next development was the provision of lightweight lifting barriers and traffic signals but the wholesale abolition of gate boxes only became possible with the introduction of remote television monitoring. This is now well under way, and by 1994 the number of signalboxes was down to eight (plus two other manned gates), compared with a one-time peak of thirtyone block posts (plus many other manned gates).

Rationalisation of signalling at the main centres on the line had already taken place. York's resignalling, planned in the late nineteen-thirties, came into effect in 1951 but the first signalbox along the Scarborough line remained Burton Lane, junction for the Foss Islands Branch. A partial rationalisation of the station layout in 1974 removed direct access from the Scarborough line to the west side of the station (platforms 14 to 16) and York Yard South, something of little consequence given the decline in freight and excursion business. 1988 saw work start on a drastic simplification of the track layout in preparation for electrification of the East Coast Main Line. The Scarborough line was singled over the Ouse Bridge and three long-disused bay platforms were abandoned at that end of the station. The signalboxes at Burton Lane and Bootham closed on 30 April 1989 and the interface with the new York signalling centre is now Strensall.

Malton, no longer a junction and having lost its engine shed, was resignalled in 1966. Malton West and the box at the station closed on 22 May, superseded by Malton East which controls the crossing on the busy Norton Road. Signalling alterations at Scarborough reflect the contraction in facilities there and it now has just the one signalbox, Falsgrave, in place of four, those lost being Gasworks (1965), Washbeck (1970) and Scarborough (the station box, in 1984), as well as Gallows Close on the Whitby line.

Following these changes, employment on the railway is a small fraction of what it used to be during the heyday of a labour-intensive operation. For example, at Malton in 1908 the North Eastern Railway employed 80 full-time staff in the passenger and goods departments.[4] This total included signalmen and other operating staff but excluded people employed at the engine shed and by the civil engineer, principally in permanent-way maintenance. Nearly all were men and many were the family breadwinner. Their importance to the local community is shown by a petition got up by local shopkeepers in January 1891 and sent

Rillington Station in 1952, showing the spidery wrought-iron skeleton of the trainshed added about 1946-7. Photo J. W. Armstrong (photographer) from the J. F. Mallon collection.

to the NER Board in response to a reorganisation of the Engineer's Department, which eventually led to eight men being moved elsewhere.[5] Now there are only three comparable railway jobs in Malton: two shifts at the signalbox and one at the booking office.

The station accommodation at Scarborough is naturally much diminished from the heyday of holiday traffic. Londesborough Road closed officially on 4 July 1966, although it had not been required for three years - the last train to use it being the 2.35 p.m. to Basford (Nottingham) on 24 August 1963. The platform roofing was subsequently removed but the platform and buildings remain.

The low-level roof over platform 2 had been demolished, in lieu of repairs, but otherwise Scarborough Central remained largely unaltered until 1970, which brought drastic surgery. The trainshed and cabstand roof were removed from platforms 1 and 2, and all that remains today is a section of the 1883 verandah roofing in front of the former excursion waiting rooms.

The short bays on the south side of the station were clearly redundant, and their removal means that regular services are now handled by the three platforms within the original trainshed. This structure has had a chequered recent history. In 1977 it was noticed that the tierods which had taken the place of the missing column at the west end were unsound and so the cast-iron arches supporting that end of the roof were replaced by a steel girder, later camouflaged to resemble its predecessor. In 1993 work was planned to thoroughly renovate the trainshed roof, including a replacement of the skylight in modern materials, but while this proposal was still making its way through the planning process another tie-rod broke and the west end of the roof was stripped of its cladding as a precaution. At the time of writing, almost two years later, appropriate repairs are still awaited.

The carriage sidings have been progressively cut back, in line with the gradual abandonment of excursion and holiday trains. First, the rundown of Londesborough Road meant there was no logic in retaining Gallows Close Sidings, then Gasworks Down were closed in favour of sidings nearer to the station.

While it is risky to speculate about the future, it is hard to visualise freight traffic ever returning to the Scarborough line but the outlook for passengers appears much more promising. In particular, the villages around York have seen a population explosion during the last two decades, chiefly as dormitory suburbs: Copmanthorpe, Haxby and Strensall being notable examples. This and the development of, currently bus-operated, park-and-ride schemes argue a case for the reinstatement of suburban train services, although employment locations are now diversified well beyond the city centre. A problem is how to provide these without unduly slowing down the present service.

It is an uncanny experience to step inside Scarborough Station on a summer Sunday and find it now a quiet backwater in the busy town. The present unimaginative fare structure makes rail travel seem very expensive compared with the perceived costs of road transport, and there is a need to recapture the commercial flair shown by the LNER during the nineteen-thirties. This is particularly important on the eve of privatisation, as costs and subsidies come again under scrutiny, and one can only hope that *Regional Railways North East,* the present operators of the service, will rise to the challenge. Whether they can do much to develop the considerably-reduced service down the coast to Hull seems more doubtful.

Table 8.1   Regular Goods Trains on the York-Scarborough line in 1953

1.   **York-Scarborough Unbraked Express Goods (Class E)**
York dep. 4.50 a.m   Scarborough arr. 6.30 a.m.

2.   **Scarborough-York Pickup Goods (serving the wayside stations)**
Scarborough dep. 8.35 a.m.

3.   **Scarborough-Gascoigne Wood Coal Train (Class F)**
Empty train: Scarborough dep. 1.30 p.m.   Gascoigne Wood arr. 4.06 p.m.
Laden: Gascoigne Wood dep 5.45 p.m.   Scarborough arr. 8.38 p.m.

4.   **Scarborough-York Braked Express Goods (Class C)**
Scarborough (Gallows Close) dep. 5.45 p.m. for Scarborough Central to attach any fish traffic.
Scarborough Central dep. 6.40 p.m.   York arr. 8.05 p.m.

Demolishing the verandah roof over Malton's up platform in October 1966. By then the engine shed had gone, though its amenity block remained as did the closed signalbox. Photo: Ken Hoole.

The decline of the pickup goods, August 1979. Diesel shunter Number 03089 has brought a single coal wagon from Scarborough out to Seamer and is shunting Seamer goods yard before heading home with four empty wagons. The shunter's truck, in front of the engine, was used to extend its effective wheelbase and so ensure its detection by track circuits. Photo: C. B. Foster.

Fletcher 2-4-0 of Class 1440, Number 1444, leaving Scarborough Station with the roof of the fish platform in the background. Hoteliers and others dependent on the holiday trade were not keen on its close and smelly proximity to the station, petitioning the NER in 1875 to resite it elsewhere. The engine has been rebuilt with a Worsdell boiler. Photo: J. F. Mallon collection.

Malton's long-lived 0-6-0 Number 1275 seen outside the east end of the shed in 1914. Photo: Ken Hoole collection.

Chapter 9

Locomotives, Accidents and Incidents

For many years the Scarborough services offered a new lease of life for North Eastern Railway express locomotives which could no longer meet the increasing demands of main line traffic. The Worsdell Singles have already been mentioned, but they were accompanied by various 4-4-0 classes and the line provided a brief final home for the North Eastern Atlantics (4-4-2's).

At first the line was probably worked by the latest York & North Midland engines but little is known of the early days other than the occasional glimpse. Thus in 1869 a special train conveying a member of the Royal Family was hauled by No. 180, a 2-2-2 originally built by Hawthorns in 1848 for the York Newcastle & Berwick Railway (and named *Plews* after a director) but rebuilt in the eighteen-sixties. During the following decade another single, No. 319, appeared at Scarborough on the first Locomotive Stores Train, and this was the YNM's *Jenny Lind,* supplied by E. B. Wilson of Leeds in 1847.

By the eighteen-eighties the use of locomotives relegated from other duties was well established, and Appendix 2 lists a selection of engines identified from E.L. Ahrons' articles in the *Railway Magazine*.[1] These were predominantly 2-4-0's although York shed operated a number of Singles. That decade is notable, however, as bringing the introduction onto regular Scarborough workings of the 4-4-0, a type commonly found on the line until almost the end of steam.

4-4-0's were already common at Malton in the form of the ten Whitby Bogies (Class 492), the only engines of this type to be designed by the NER's first Locomotive Superintendent, Edward Fletcher, and introduced in 1864 to work the difficult route to Whitby. The last was withdrawn in 1893, a modest record compared with the 0-6-0 based at Malton until February 1923 to work the pickup goods to Whitby. This was Number 1275, built in 1874 and the last survivor of the once-numerous Class 1001 which originated on the Stockton & Darlington Railway. After withdrawal it ran in the 1925 Railway Centenary procession and is now to be found at North Road Station Museum in Darlington.

The first 4-4-0 to take on the passenger service to Scarborough was the Class 38, designed by Fletcher's short-lived successor, Alexander McDonnell. Introduced in 1884 they were remarkably unpopular and, quickly displaced from main-line duties, a number found their way to Scarborough, where they were regularly seen on trains to York and Leeds and were soon joined by their successors, T. W. Worsdell's Class F (LNER Class D22).

Dating from 1887, the Worsdell engines were beginning to be edged off the East Coast Expresses within six years by their larger cousins of Class M, but the lines from Scarborough to Leeds and Hull were well suited to their abilities and by the end of the century they were the most common passenger engine on the line, far more so than their exact contemporaries of Class G1 - a 4-4-0 specifically designed for use on secondary routes. For a time the fast-running Singles (4-2-2's) of Classes I and J seem to have monopolised the faster trains, with the J's producing some splendid performances on the non-stop express as described in Chapter 6, but the First World War put an end to their brief spell of glory and they were scrapped shortly afterwards. The F's, by contrast, lasted into the nineteen-thirties although their duties had been downgraded by the appearance of the larger 4-4-0's designed by T. W. Worsdell's successor, his brother Wilson.

These were classes M and Q (both LNER Class D17). The former tended to work the coast route into Scarborough from a base at Hull, although the majority ended their days at Bridlington shed. The Q's took over the Leeds service and seem to have been the mainstay of this in the decade following the First World War but most were withdrawn during the nineteen-thirties, having been displaced by the North Eastern's penultimate design of 4-4-0: Class R (D20).

Wilson Worsdell's Class R was the North Eastern's finest 4-4-0 design. Built between 1899 and 1907, these engines were employed on main-line duties for over twenty years before being displaced to secondary routes. By the end of 1927 Scarborough shed had four, working the Leeds expresses in conjunction with engines from Neville Hill shed (Leeds) and the fast trains on the coast line to Hull, while 1932 saw their numbers up to seven.

In 1934 the unthinkable happened and Scarborough shed actually received a batch of brand new passenger engines, fresh

D20 (NER Class R) being turned at Scarborough shed in July 1953. Photo: J. F. Mallon collection.

Malton Shed coaling stage with Worsdell Class A 2-4-2T Number 1580, which worked passenger trains to Whitby for many years. Photo: Ken Hoole collection.

from Darlington Works. These were the second version of Nigel Gresley's 4-4-0's of Class D49, the *Hunts*, designed specifically for express duties on secondary routes in the North Eastern and Scottish Areas of the LNER. Despite a reputation for rough riding they put in good work, replacing the D20's on the principal trains and, with one break, operating the line for twentyfive years. 1939 brought another batch of remaindered main-line locomotives in the form of Wilson Worsdell's Class V Atlantics (LNER C6), but the outbreak of War led to a further reshuffle. The Atlantics vanished in March 1940, while the fall in holiday traffic brought the removal of the D49's to heavier duties elsewhere in May 1941. Their place was taken by the faithful D20's but within two years Scarborough had regained a pair of D49's.

Following the end of hostilities, in 1945, there was a further rationalisation, aimed at minimising the variety of classes at each shed. Scarborough lost all its D20's to Selby and received instead eight Atlantics of Vincent Raven's Class Z (LNER C7), introduced in 1911. Displaced from second-rank main-line duties by Gresley's V2's these once-fine engines had become candidates for scrapping even before the War. They were badly run down on arrival and, although revived by the attentions of Scarborough shed staff, were quite inappropriate for the duties required there.

In the Summer of 1948 the D49's returned in force and Scarborough's Atlantics were speedily despatched to the scrapyard, the last to go being (B.R. number) 62992 which left in November; a month later the whole class had been withdrawn. The D49's put in another decade as the mainstay of passenger services on the line until two classes of modern 4-6-0 made an appearance as fugitives from dieselisation. Four of British Railways Standard Class 5 arrived at Scarborough shed in January 1959 but were despatched in June to make way for something closer to North Eastern traditions, three of Edward Thompson's B1's. One of the last classes introduced by the LNER, they were already a familiar sight at Scarborough working in from other depots but did not remain long, being sent away in March 1960 on the introduction of diesel multiple units. Scarborough's last D49 was Number 62762, which remained there until withdrawn in October 1960.

For many years the slower stopping trains in the North East were handled by 0-4-4 tank locomotives, first the set of variations on a Fletcher theme known as BTP: Bogie Tank Passenger (LNER G6), and then Wilson Worsdell's long-lived Class O (G5). At the end of the nineteenth century BTP's still predominated at Scarborough, with Class O just beginning to make an appearance. In 1905, following the success of an experiment at Hartlepool, the NER converted a number of BTP's for autocar (push and pull) working in conjunction with a coach having a driving compartment at the far end, and one such unit was used to augment the stopping service from York as far as Strensall.

By comparison with passenger services, and in marked contrast to other parts of the NER system, goods trains were relatively thin on the ground and normally were hauled by 0-6-0's. At the turn of the century the most common at Scarborough were Edward Fletcher's 398 Class but these were supplanted by Worsdell designs. By the nineteen-twenties, the largest of these, the powerful P3 (LNER Class J27), were regularly engaged on the York-Scarborough goods, with their smaller brethren working the pickup. The coal trains, working from Gascoigne Wood Yard via York, were more demanding and the North Eastern 0-8-0's of classes T1 and T2 (LNER Q5 and Q6) were brought onto these, followed in the nineteen-thirties by the NER's largest mixed traffic locomotive, Vincent Raven's 4-6-0 of Class S3 (LNER Class B16).

Introduced in 1919, the B16's were very effective machines, often called on to handle the heavier holiday trains and happily taking twelve coaches from Leeds to Scarborough. In January 1930 Scarborough shed received its first B16, number 845, which remained there until called away to war service in 1943. While its weekday task was to work the coal train, at weekends it was available for relief work. After the War another B16, number 61445, went to Scarborough to resume these duties and remained there until its withdrawal in July 1961.

A variety of engines were used as station pilots, a very important task during busy periods at Scarborough; during the nineteen-thirties these were J21 0-6-0's (T.W. Worsdell's Class C). Fifty years old, they made an interesting contrast with the locomotive eventually adopted as the *coal pilot,* whose duties included ferrying wagons to Scarborough Gasworks; this was the J72 0-6-0 tank engine number 69016, newly built by British Railways in January 1950 to a Worsdell design dating from 1898.

Much of the fascination of Scarborough's trains lay in the

G5 (NER Class O) waiting to leave Scarborough's platform 6 with a typical NER clerestory carriage, in the early nineteen-thirties. The two arches in the background carry the two-bay extension to the main trainshed carried out in 1859, and were encased in masonry almost thirty years later. Photo: Ken Hoole collection.

amazing variety of engines seen on holiday services. Before the 1923 grouping there were regular workings by the Great Northern, Great Central, Great Eastern, Midland, Lancashire & Yorkshire and London & North Western Railways, although the last gave up through working in 1904. The *foreign* crews worked through to Scarborough but took on a North Eastern driver as pilotman at York, while a NER guard took charge of the train. Grouping did little to alter this scene, other than to bring a reduction in the variety of locomotive and carriage liveries.

A wide range of locomotive classes was still to be seen after nationalisation, with one important development. During the nineteen-thirties it had been impractical to work the largest LNER locomotives through to Scarborough because of the restricted size of its turntables, and the appearance there of Gresley Pacific number 2795 *Call Boy* on 17 July 1937 must have been something of an embarrassment. It had brought a Glasgow train via the Pilmoor-Malton line and had to be despatched to York tender-first, working empty coaching stock. The provision of a triangular junction at the new Filey Holiday Camp station solved the problem, so the British Railways era eventually saw Gresley's V2 2-6-2's, a variety of LNER Pacifics and even the B.R. standard *Britannias* appearing in town.

An insight into locomotive operation on the NER is provided by the rosters for Scarborough shed in 1891, at which time there were 16 passenger duties divided into 3 *links*: Number 1 with ten turns all to York and Leeds, Number 2 with two turns to Hull, and Number 3 with four trips to Saltburn and Pickering. The run to Leeds and back, 137 miles, was then a day's work but on the Hull trips the engines fitted in other workings during the stopover at Hull. One ran to Hornsea while the other performed a return trip to Bridlington. The latter gave the longest mileage and hours of any of the Scarborough workings: 169.5 miles and 15 hours. The engine and crew left Scarborough at 8.30 a.m. and were not due back until 9.40 p.m.

Long hours were common under the NER but the utilisation of locomotives and crew then, and for many years afterwards, was poor and often little more than half the time was actually spent in motion. In contrast, excursion train crews could spend enormously long periods on the footplate, the most extreme Scarborough example on record being the Great Eastern crew which worked a Bass special from London on 15 June 1894.[2] This conveyed the men who worked in the beer store under St.

Pancras Station and entailed a run of 265 miles each way, including the empty-stock workings to and from Stratford. This was felt to be too far for a coal-fired locomotive to cope with, because of the build up of ash and clinker, so the Great Eastern Railway won the contract with an oil-fired 2-4-0, number 761 of James Holden's T19 class, which was usually employed on the Royal trains to Sandringham.

The empty stock left Stratford just after 5 a.m. for St. Pancras, from which a punctual departure was made at 6. The train then proceeded over the Great Eastern to Cambridge and March and the Great Northern & Great Eastern Joint Line, via Lincoln, to Doncaster; it then followed the normal route through York to Scarborough. Stops were made to take on water at Ely, Lincoln and Selby and it was getting on for midday when the train reached Scarborough. The crew were booked for nine hours rest before setting off again at 9 p.m. but the attractions of the town proved too much and when the train finally rolled into St. Pancras about 3 a.m. they were so tired they could barely stand up.

Although regular dmu services on the Leeds-Scarborough route only began in 1960, the NER was the first British railway to build petrol powered railcars, in 1903. August 1904 saw one of these make its debut at Scarborough on a Summer service to Filey. During 1906 and 1907 it proved too small for the traffic and its afternoon working was taken over by a BTP autocar, while it ran instead to Forge Valley, on the Pickering Branch. In 1908 it was despatched to the less-demanding Cawood and Selby line.

After the First World War the NER returned to the internal combustion engine to power the York-Strensall local service. In 1922 a Leyland motorbus was converted to run on rails; seating 26 passengers it began operation on 19 July. This was a temporary expedient to establish a more frequent service, in competition with road buses, and on 21 September Vincent Raven was authorised to spend £2500 on building a *rail-motor* coach. Equipped with a 105 horsepower Daimler engine and seating forty third-class in a single saloon, it emerged from York Carriage Works in July 1923 as LNER Number 2105Y. Taking over from the Leyland railbus on 9 July, it worked an expanded local service until the closure of the wayside stations in 1930.

During 1924 the LNER conducted trials of two Sentinel steam railcars, the ultimate test being a run from York to Whitby via Pickering, returning by the coast to Scarborough and York. The

Sentinel steam railcar Number 2236 "British Queen" leaving Scarborough's platform 7 probably for Pickering, via the Forge Valley line. It is hauling an LNER lightweight trailer carriage. Photo: Lens of Sutton.

successful outcome led to the purchase of 80 railcars up to 1932, their first regular appearance in Scarborough being that of the Pickering-based *Rodney,* operating on the Forge Valley line from 11 April 1928. Subsequently they became a common sight on the Whitby lines and also operated on the Ryedale line out of Malton until it lost its passenger service at the end of 1930. Most were withdrawn during the War, the last being scrapped in 1948.

Diesel traction made its first appearance at Scarborough in February 1933 when the Middlesbrough-based diesel-electric railcar *Tyneside Venturer* began working in from Saltburn. A prototype vehicle built by Armstrong Whitworth at Scotswood on Tyne, from 17 July it worked a daily Summer Scenic Tour from Scarborough to Whitby via Pickering, returning along the coast for a fare of 5 shillings (25p). This was repeated in successive Summers up to 1938 when the railcar was becoming very unreliable; it was withdrawn after minor collision damage in May 1939.

Despite the short life of *Tyneside Venturer* compared with the Sentinel railcars, the LNER would have experimented further with diesel traction had it not been for the War and nationalisation. In the event it was to be almost twenty years before diesels returned to Scarborough with the advent of Craven-built dmu's on the coast line from Hull on 29 July 1957, followed by the Middlesbrough service on 5 May 1958 and the York service two years later. The dmu's did a lot to ease the working of Scarborough Station, eliminating the problems of engines running round their trains or propelling them into platforms but locomotive-hauled trains, with their attendant problems, were still very common during the summer.

Diesel locomotives were late in making an appearance, the first being Number D252 (English Electric Type 4) which worked into Scarborough on 21 July 1960 on a driver training trip in the charge of Inspector Charlie Fisher; 37 years earlier he had fired the NER Pacific Number 2400 in its comparative trials against Gresley's A1.

For most of the steam era the lives of engine crews held some unpleasant hazards, as on 22 April 1861 when a Scarborough-York express was derailed about a mile west of Malton. The engine ran down the low embankment, across a ditch and into a field where it *turned clear over.* Though the line was not particularly accident prone, only 4 years later there was a collision at Malton. The inquiry elicited a revealing catalogue of the duties of the porter-signalman involved:

- 6 a.m. Begin duty and sweep out a train
- Fetch lamp from York *back signal*
- Look to water closets and clean them
- Breakfast
- Attend to signals
- Attend to passenger trains as porter
- After the passage of the 10.10am to York, wash the Driffield train.
- 11am Attend to signals again
- Shunt Driffield train at 11.50am.
- Attend to signals until 1pm.
- 1pm to 2pm Dinner
- Attend to signals
- Clean and couple Driffield train and shunt it out at 4.30pm
- Light signal lamps
- Leave after passage of last train from York, about 8 p.m.

For all this he received seventeen shillings (85p) per week. Although in attendance for passenger trains, he was often busy with other duties when goods trains were approaching so they got into the habit of running in without signals.

With the adoption of block signalling in 1873 and the recruitment of many more signalmen train working improved but mishaps continued to occur. Excursions posed their own problems as on 6 July 1869 when two excursions from Doncaster were combined at York to form a train of 31 carriages conveying a thousand passengers. Despite three brakevans it was unable to stop at Castle Howard and collided with a goods train. Two years later there was the opposite problem at Kirkham Abbey when the engine and train of an L&Y excursion parted company; it was said that the North Eastern guard had applied the brake too suddenly. More typical was the breakdown of locomotives on Summer Saturdays, with traffic queueing up behind, although disabled steam engines could generally be relied on to limp on to the end of their journey.

The pickup goods, shunting wagons at the wayside stations, faced a particular hazard since sidings in country goods yards were not a maintenance priority, and so railwaymen had to be adept at rerailing. The signalbox occurrence book for Ganton reveals that the goods engine, in turn a J21, J24 and J25, became

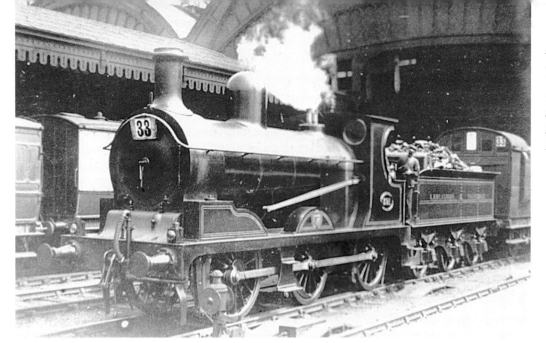

A Lancashire & Yorkshire Railway excursion to Scarborough before the First World War. An Aspinall 0-6-0 heads its train, probably from East Lancashire, along the through lines in the centre of York Station. Photo: C.B. Foster collection (per I.G. Storey).

The River Derwent invading Malton Station and engine shed during the 1947 floods. Photo: J. F. Mallon collection.

derailed in the station sidings three times in the period 1928-32; on no occasion did it take longer than twenty minutes to rerail.

Things could be much more serious, however, and at Scarborough, with its congested layout and many shunting movements, there was ample scope for accidents. A particular problem was the attempt to expedite station working by having train engines propel (i.e. push) their carriages into the platforms. On 16 March 1883, a Pickering-Scarborough train was waiting at the ticket platform near Falsgrave signalbox, while the train engine prepared to run around it prior to propelling the carriages into a platform. Unfortunately the driver misread the signals, the points had not yet been changed and he drove straight into his own train. Two years later, on 16 August, the engine off the 4.20 a.m. mail from York was propelling its train into a platform when it collided with two empty carriages which were already standing there. At the resulting inquiry it was recommended that this practice be abandoned, yet at busy times the stationmaster still felt obliged to authorise it, but after a similar accident in August 1891 the NER issued instructions that it should cease immediately.

The assumption was that the men driving the station pilot engines were better able to judge platform lengths than visiting drivers but even this broke down on 10 December 1891 when a set of carriages was routed into the wrong platform. It should have entered Platform 4 but was despatched instead into Platform 3, already occupied by the stock for the 10.40 a.m. to York. Fortunately, the only passengers to have taken their seats were two ladies who were uninjured and continued their journey. The results were dramatic enough, with the rear carriage being pushed over the buffers and through the rear wall of the trainshed.

Where injuries occurred, these were usually to railwaymen. Thus on 17 March 1915 the guard of a Whitby-Scarborough train was killed by his train's engine, a Class O tank (LNER G5) while changing the tail lamp; it was supposed to be running round the carriages but the wrong signal lever had been pulled and it hit them instead. A sense of responsibility could also take its toll as with the driver of a D20 (Number 2014) which failed to stop on time in Platform 2 on 18 July 1935. The engine hit the buffers, coming to rest on the platform, and the driver was so upset that he committed suicide a few days later.

Scarborough's worst accident came during the Second World War and arose from the sort of understandable human error which no system can entirely eliminate. On 10 August 1943 a signalman in the station box mistakenly routed an incoming train into Platform 5, which was already occupied by the coaching stock of a train for Hull.[3] The driver of the engine, D20 Number 2024, was unable to stop in time and it wrecked the first three coaches of the standing train, occupied by a detachment of soldiers, four of whom were killed. There were no casualties on the incoming train. The accident happened at 10.57 a.m., the last injured person was rescued at 12.35 and the platform reopened three hours later. Signalman Scholes took full reponsibility for his mistake and, haunted by its consequences, died just a few years later.

Fortunately, nothing comparable has happened since then. Level crossings inevitably give rise to occasional incidents while stock can cause problems, as at Barton Hill in May 1969 when fire broke out in the toilet compartment of a dmu and passengers had to be escorted up to the level crossing while the delinquent carriage was uncoupled and left to burn out.

B16 (NER Class S3) Number 1380 arriving at York on a train from Scarborough in June 1933. On the left is Waterworks Box, with the railway waterworks, complete with tank, behind it. Photo: H. Madgewick, J. F. Mallon collection.

Chapter 10

Down the Line to Scarborough

GENERAL NOTE: *The station diagrams in this chapter are based on NER and LNER Siding Diagrams from the period 1905-35. Unless otherwise stated they can be assumed to represent the station layout from 1914 until wholesale surgery began in 1965.*

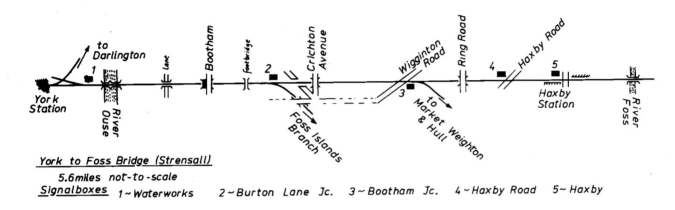

Line Diagram: York-Foss Bridge.

1. York to Foss Bridge (Strensall)

The original line left the Great North of England Railway by a junction which entailed trains from York reversing, presumably they were drawn out of the station by a pilot engine. It then entered a shallow cutting spanned by Thief Lane Bridge and passed a group of cottages and the railway's waterworks before crossing the Ouse. The cottages comprised a standard YNM terrace together with a pair of NER houses added in 1861.[1] In 1862 four were occupied by foremen at railway workshops and the engine shed while the other housed the engineman at the waterworks, where the NER's supply was pumped up from the river.

A decade later these houses were demolished to make way for York's new station but the waterworks remained, giving its name to a signalbox and the crossing by which goods lines from York Yard South made their way across the East Coast Main Line to reach the Scarborough Branch. Waterworks Box was demolished in 1938, in connection with station extensions, and replaced by a temporary box which survived until the 1951 resignalling.

Once over the Ouse, the line crosses the buried viaduct, passing the site of the ticket platform before entering a cutting and heading beneath Bootham, the main road to the North. Brick retaining walls, capped with handsome cast-iron railings, step back to accommodate the platforms and access steps of Bootham Station. These were never built but the cast-iron deck intended to carry the booking office remains, bearing an electricity substation, alongside the rebuilt reinforced concrete deck of the roadbridge.

The start of the line. J27 (NER Class P3) Number 1366 heads a goods train from York Yard South across the East Coast Main Line at Waterworks Box onto the Scarborough Branch. The Scarborough passenger lines are in the foreground. Photo: C.B. Foster collection (per I.G. Storey).

Haxby Station before the First World War with an autotrain waiting to leave for York. The cattle dock is in the centre and the wagons to its left are standing on the coal depot. Photo: Lens of Sutton.

Beyond this the railway skirts the spacious grounds of Bootham Park Hospital, screened by an impressive line of trees, whose leaf fall now causes wheelslip and track-circuit problems for the lightweight Sprinter trains. At the end of the hospital grounds, the unmanned crossing at Asylum Lane gave way to a NER covered footbridge, a popular route to Bootham Crescent football ground, replaced by the present concrete structure in 1962.

A mile from the line's datum point in the centre of York Station we come to the site of Burton Lane Junction. Originally just a level crossing, it became the junction for the Foss Islands Branch, built by the NER under pressure from York Corporation to serve the Cattle Market. This carried traffic from 8 December 1879 until the Autumn of 1988. At one time Foss Islands Depot supplied sand to the glassworks in Fishergate, while there were sidings to the gasworks, electric power station, Rowntree's chocolate factory and the railway laundry.[2] There was a link to the Derwent Valley Light Railway and from November 1927 the branch carried a workmen's service to Rowntree's Halt. Now its route is a footpath and cycleway.

Burton Lane (later Burtonstone Lane) was the second level crossing to be replaced by a roadbridge (the first being Musham Bank near Seamer), under an agreement confirmed by the LNER Traffic Committee on 23 October 1930. This was paid for by York Corporation, who were developing houses beyond the railway and built Crichton Avenue to link up with them.[3] They also took over the LNER's responsibility for maintaining the roadway on the bridge carrying Wigginton Road over the Foss Islands Branch.

The first level crossing today is over Wigginton Road, once the site of Bootham Junction, where a line took off for Hull. Another Hudson venture, this opened on 4 October 1847 as far as Market Weighton but the more difficult section through the Wolds was deferred and only completed to join the coast line at Beverley eighteen years later. Its closure in 1965 was arguably one of Beeching's less wise decisions. Though its annual income of £90,400 was set against operating expenses of £150,800, the deficit could have been drastically reduced by adopting the sort of economies soon to be practised on other routes.[4] Renamed Bootham, the box closed on 30 April 1989 under the York resignalling.

The crossing is the site of the makeshift Bootham Station opened in 1848 to serve the Royal (Agricultural) Show on Bootham Stray, and local tradition lays claim to a platform though there is no confirmation of this on any maps. Continuing across the Stray, with a speed limit of 70mph, the line passes under York's northern bypass, begun in 1984, to Haxby. At Haxby Road Crossing, on the main road from York, is the first surviving YNM terrace together with a good example of a G. T. Andrews' crossing cottage.

Haxby Station lies almost a mile from the centre of the village. The station house is an elegant G. T. Andrews' design, with a prominent Farnese Palace doorcase, extended early on to provide an extra bedroom above the waiting room. The first down platform would have been a low, flagged area in front of the house but when the NER came to install longer and higher platforms, in line with Board of Trade demands, it was moved to the opposite side of the crossing. Thus the engines of waiting trains no longer obstructed the road, and similar staggered platforms were installed at Strensall and Kirkham Abbey. Had a 1912 scheme gone ahead, Haxby might have come to greater prominence as the junction of a light railway to Brandsby.[5]

Between Haxby and Strensall there is little of note other than the crossing of the former Foss Navigation by a modest girder bridge of three spans, extensively rebuilt.

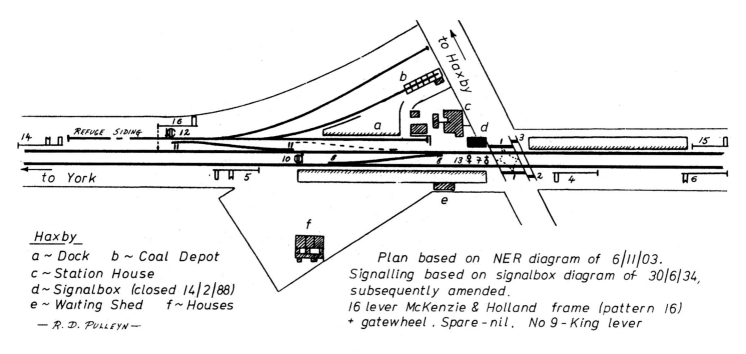

Haxby

a ~ Dock   b ~ Coal Depot
c ~ Station House
d ~ Signalbox (closed 14/2/88)
e ~ Waiting Shed   f ~ Houses

— R. D. PULLEYN —

Plan based on NER diagram of 6/11/03.
Signalling based on signalbox diagram of 30/6/34,
subsequently amended.
16 lever McKenzie & Holland frame (pattern 16)
+ gatewheel . Spare - nil. No 9 - King lever

Station Diagram: Haxby. Courtesy R. D. Pulleyn

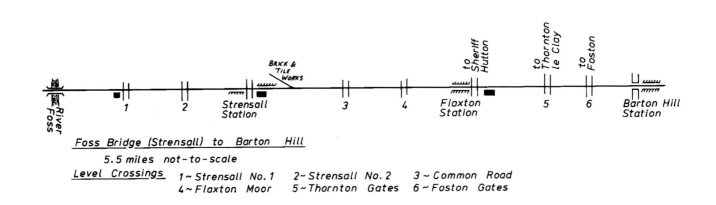

Foss Bridge (Strensall) to Barton Hill

5.5 miles not-to-scale

Level Crossings   1 ~ Strensall No.1   2 ~ Strensall No.2   3 ~ Common Road
4 ~ Flaxton Moor   5 ~ Thornton Gates   6 ~ Foston Gates

Line Diagram: Foss Bridge-Barton Hill.

2. Foss Bridge (Strensall) to Barton Hill

Once in Strensall there are two level crossings before reaching the station. Strensall Number 2 is the site of a halt opened in connection with the railbus service introduced in 1922. First shown in the timetable for 19 July 1926, it lasted only four more years.

Strensall Station lies quite close to the centre of the village, and the nearby late-Victorian houses suggest a modest growth stimulated by the railway. Industry took the form of Littlethorpe Brick and Tile Company, served by a siding installed in 1901 and despatching over a thousand tons of bricks a year by rail prior to the First World War.[6] Now the brickworks has vanished under housing, the village having become, with Haxby, one of York's major commuting resorts - by car. The signalbox, the first now surviving on the line, dates from 1901 and is a good example of that period. Other crossings with automatic barriers are monitored by television from here.

In 1876 the War Office, then building an infantry barracks at York, purchased over two square miles of Strensall Common for training. This brought considerable traffic during the First World War, with passenger bookings in 1915 reaching an all-time peak of 149,303, five times the prewar average. Strensall Camp also ensured continued business after the withdrawal of regular passenger services in 1930 with, for example, 5,149 passengers booked during 1935 and a surge of activity during the Second World War.

A mile beyond the station the line enters the woodland of Strensall Common, one of few surviving fragments of the ancient Forest of Galtres. Further on, Common Lane Crossing forms a period piece with its YNM gate cottage and former platelayers' houses alongside an LNER prefabricated concrete gatekeeper's cabin. It is a quiet spot and, in accordance with the practice originally adopted on all but turnpike roads, the gates are normally kept shut against road traffic. The crossing is manned every day of the year. The next one is Flaxton Moor, with an original but uncharacteristic two-storey gatehouse.

Flaxton is a very small village straggling along one side of a road but its station was a railhead for other communities, such as Sheriff Hutton, hence the nearby Thompson's Arms Hotel, which appears contemporary with the railway. Once a month Flaxton used to be a venue for Bulmer East Petty Sessions and the NER helpfully allowed the 10.40 a.m. Scarborough-York express to stop there when the magistrates required. As most of them lived in York, this must have been for the NER's former Southern Division Engineer, Harold Copperthwaite, who retired to Scarborough but continued to serve on the Bench.[7]

As a significant agricultural railhead, Flaxton had a potato dock, despatching just over a thousand tons of potatoes in 1923, and a goods shed (something not found at either Haxby or Strensall). A YNM structure, like that at Seamer, it survived an accident in August 1867 when a passenger train to Scarborough collided with an up goods which had been shunted onto the down line to allow an up passenger train to pass. The passenger engine finished up on its side, taking with it one of the shed's cast-iron columns.

Beyond Flaxton we pass Thornton Gates and Foston Gates, both now reduced to pedestrian crossings and the former having lost both its gatehouse and platelayers' terrace.

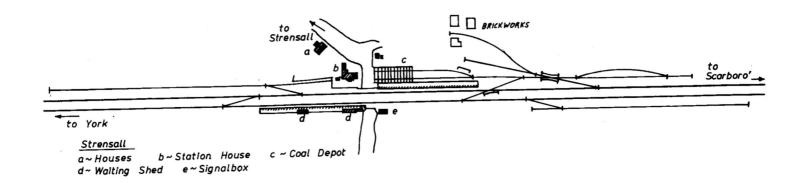

Station Diagram: Strensall.

to Strensall

BRICKWORKS

to Scarboro'

to York

<u>Strensall</u>

a ~ Houses   b ~ Station House   c ~ Coal Depot

d ~ Waiting Shed   e ~ Signalbox

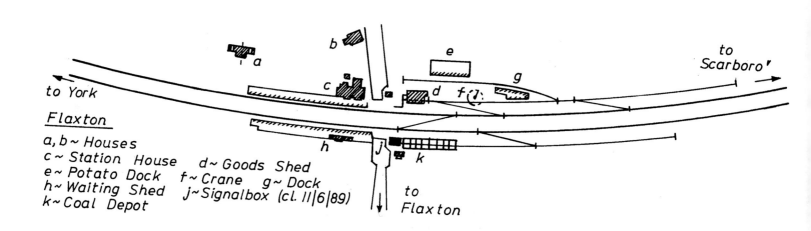

Station Diagram: Flaxton.

to Scarboro'

to York

<u>Flaxton</u>

a, b ~ Houses

c ~ Station House   d ~ Goods Shed

e ~ Potato Dock   f ~ Crane   g ~ Dock

h ~ Waiting Shed   J ~ Signalbox (cl. 11/6/89)

k ~ Coal Depot

to Flaxton

Strensall Number 2 Crossing in the nineteen-fifties. In front of the modest gatebox is the short platform built in connection with the railmotor service in the nineteen-twenties. The train is heading for York behind a rather grubby B1, Number 61318. Photo: J. F. Sedgewick.

Strensall Station with a stopping train waiting at the down platform. Just to its left, behind the signal, are wagons waiting on the coal depot. Photo: Lens of Sutton.

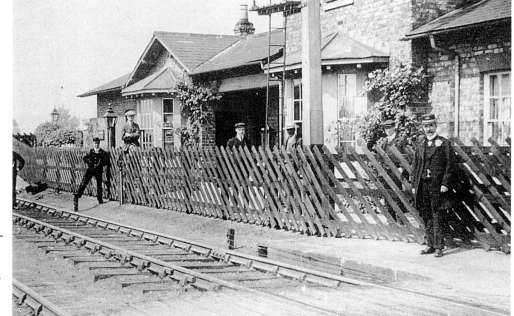

Flaxton Station. Part of the original down platform paving can be glimpsed in front of the signal post while the ramp of the later NER - platform just creeps into the left of this view. The stationmaster is seen on the right, with floral buttonhole, together with the handful of staff needed to run a small country station in NER days. Photo: J. F. Mallon collection.

A NER period scene at Barton Hill Station. Photo: J.F. Mallon collection.

The distinctive LNER signalbox at Barton Hill, with the wheel-operated lifting barrier to the left and a modern tubular post signal to the right. Photo: Bill Fawcett.

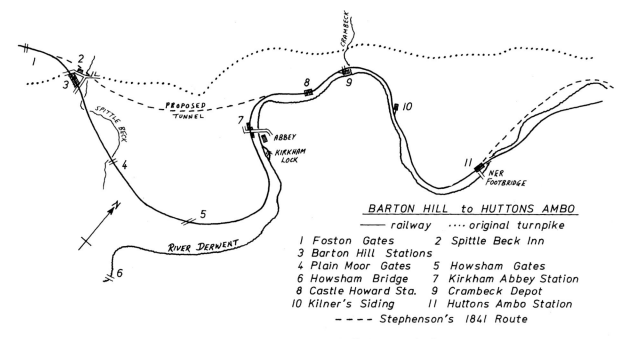

BARTON HILL to HUTTONS AMBO

——— railway   ···· original turnpike

1 Foston Gates   2 Spittle Beck Inn
3 Barton Hill Stations
4 Plain Moor Gates   5 Howsham Gates
6 Howsham Bridge   7 Kirkham Abbey Station
8 Castle Howard Sta.   9 Crambeck Depot
10 Kilner's Siding   11 Huttons Ambo Station
— — — — Stephenson's 1841 Route

Line Diagram: Barton Hill-Huttons Ambo.

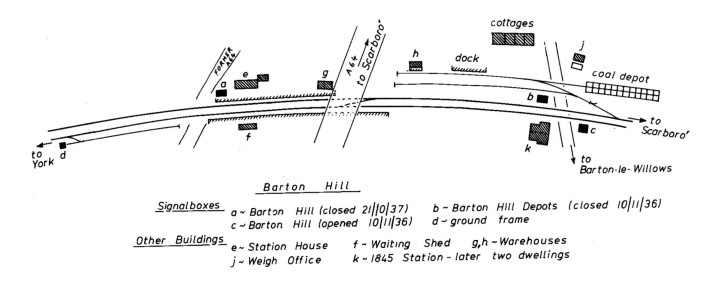

Barton Hill

Signalboxes a ~ Barton Hill (closed 21|10|37)   b ~ Barton Hill Depots (closed 10|11|36)
             c ~ Barton Hill (opened 10|11|36)   d ~ ground frame

Other Buildings e ~ Station House   f ~ Waiting Shed   g,h ~ Warehouses
                 j ~ Weigh Office   k ~ 1845 Station - later two dwellings

Station Diagram: Barton Hill.

3. Barton Hill to Huttons Ambo

At Barton Hill there were two level crossings, just a few hundred yards apart, one over the turnpike (A64) and the other over the road to Barton-le-Willows, a mile distant. The first station was built at the Barton crossing but replaced almost immediately by one at the turnpike, and by March 1850 the YNM were seeking to let the former station house. It is very similar to Haxby and was eventually converted into two dwellings for signalmen; its replacement is a nondescript affair formed by enlarging the original crossing cottage.

There was a signalbox at each crossing, an extravagance resolved by the North Riding County Council when they chose to dual this stretch of the A64 and bridge the railway. In 1936 the council agreed to pay for alterations to the goods yard, bisected by the new road, and a new signalbox at the Barton crossing, which remained.[8] They also provided steps from the new bridge to the down platform of the defunct station and agreed to do the same for the other platform as well if it ever reopened. The bridge girders were erected on 13 September 1936 and the new signalbox came into use on 10 November. The old one was then retained as a gatebox until the closure of the level crossing on 21 October 1937. This left the historic Spital Bridge Inn stranded alongside a dead-end road and its licence was later transferred to a new roadhouse on the A64.

The present Barton Hill signalbox is an interesting example of LNER design. When it first opened there were two sets of crossing gates, one pair operated from the customary gatewheel inside the box. The other protected the station sidings and had no remote control. So, when the sidings were being shunted, the signalman had to close the main gates across the road and then walk down to the others and secure them by hand; fortunately there was not much road traffic.[6] Following the removal of the sidings in 1965, the signalman's burden was eased by the installation of an early type of lightweight lifting barrier, still mechanically operated, with a hinged *skirt* hanging from the boom.

While the A64 heads straight up Whitwell Hill, the railway sweeps round towards the Derwent, crossing a minor road from Crambe to Howsham, Hudson's birthplace. The YNM terrace here is built, unusually, of stone though the gatehouse is an ordinary brick design and suggestions that it served occasionally as a station seem unjustified. Continuing towards Kirkham the line almost doubles back on itself to enter the gap through the Howardian Hills, the bend restricting train speeds to 45 mph even for Sprinters.

Kirkham Abbey is a noted beauty spot, taking its name from the substantial priory ruins situated on the east bank of the river alongside the weir which has replaced the Kirkham Lock of the Derwent Navigation. During the nineteenth century the railway fostered a traffic in visitors coming to walk, fish or boat on the Derwent and an enterprising signalman, Mr. Lazenby, offered rowing boats for hire. This led to some unusual freight traffic, as in 1926 when the railway conveyed a lifeboat from the liner *Mauretania* to Kirkham for conversion to a river cruiser. The stationmaster also had a sideline: as well as the usual coal business he operated a sub post-office, as happened at a few of the other stations.

The station house is an enlarged version of the Haxby design, built from local limestone, significantly altered in recent years and now a cafe and garden centre. In an attractive riverside setting are two well-conserved blocks of railway houses, one YNM and the other a much-extended NER signalman's house of 1873-4. The small-paned sashes of the earlier houses are very distinctive. The signalbox dates from 1873 and the introduction of block signalling, and is a fine example of the NER Southern Division design of that period.

For most of the way from Kirkham Abbey to Huttons Ambo there was formerly a 40mph speed limit as the railway squeezes between the hillside and the ever-winding Derwent. After almost a mile we reach Castle Howard Station, which was a public station reached by a private road through the Castle Howard Estate. It is a handsome, one-off Italianate building though related to the standard Haxby design. From the earliest days horse-buses were provided to convey sightseers to Vanbrugh's great mansion. The most notable passenger was Queen Victoria who stayed at Castle Howard before setting off in the Royal Train to open Newcastle Central Station and the Royal Border Bridge on 29 August 1850.[9] The estate is thickly wooded here and at one stage this caused problems with drivers' sighting of signals round the bends. In March 1860 the NER received permission to fell some trees to clear the view, in return they paid compensation for the timber and an annual fee of £2.50 in consideration of the ground remaining unplanted.

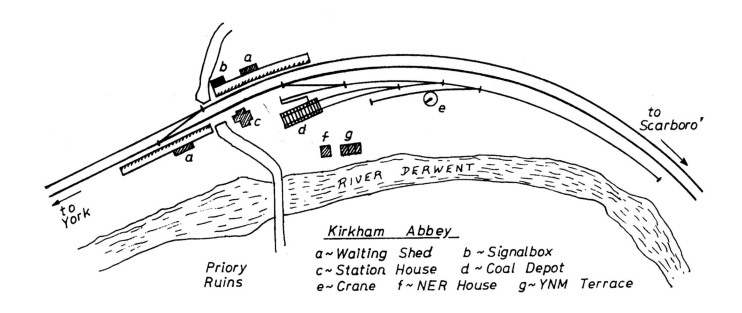

Station Diagram: Kirkham Abbey.

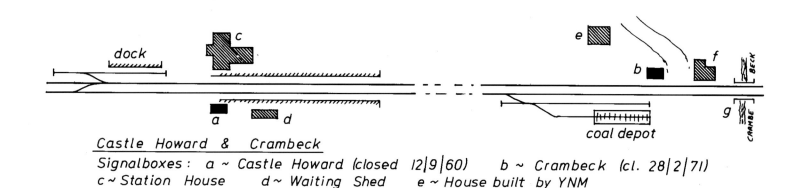

Station Diagram: Castle Howard and Crambeck.

Kirkham Abbey Station, looking east in NER days. Note the 15 mile post just before the crossing and the staggered platforms. These are of the final NER type, corbelled out to meet Board of Trade demands for a refuge between the platform wall and the track. The nameboard is a standard NER enamelled-iron one, unlike that at Barton Hill. Photo: Lens of Sutton.

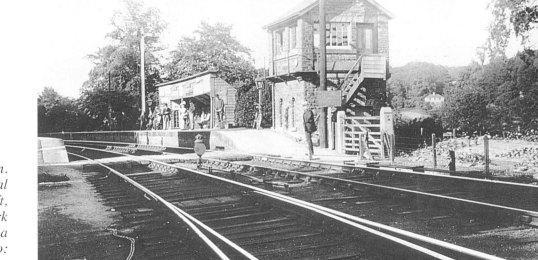

Castle Howard Station, looking towards Malton. To the right of the signalbox is the ornamental garden, complete with fountain. To its left, passengers are standing around the original York & North Midland waiting shed, which became a holiday cottage after the station's closure. Photo: Lens of Sutton.

The distinctive station building at Castle Howard. Photo: Ken Hoole collection.

It would have been insensitive to locate coal cells and other goods facilities here; instead there was just a dock, probably intended for horses, carriages and luggage. The coal depot for Castle Howard was a quarter mile further down the line at Crambeck and was much older than the railway, having been served originally by the Navigation. Even there the Earl of Carlisle's amenities were carefully considered. It was necessary to demolish an estate house to make way for the railway, and this may be the origin of the Gothic dwelling which stands just above the line. It is a typical G.T. Andrews design, in a Gothic style which he later used on the Whitby Branch but which is unique on the Scarborough line. The crossing only served the depot and originally had no gatehouse but, after discussions with the Earl's agent, one was built in 1857 at a cost of £159. Designed by the NER architect, Thomas Prosser, it also is a deliberately picturesque building, quite distinct from any of the company's standard designs.

Crossing Crambe Beck by a brick arch, the line continues towards Huttons Ambo, passing the site of a short siding and loading stage. Kilner's Siding served an industrial sand quarry operated by the Castle Howard Sand Company, later part of the Sand, Glass & Foundry Materials Company. In 1913 the Burythorpe Sand Company had plans for a light railway branching off nearby but the First World War put an end to that.[10]

The name Huttons Ambo refers to the two Huttons, High and Low, the station being situated naturally in the latter, down by the river. There were no coal cells, just a loading dock. The station buildings are the only single-storey design on the branch to remain substantially unaltered, extensions having been made by a two-storey block added at the rear.

The line crosses the Derwent on the rebuilt bridge and then skirts the river meadows, with the speed limit now eased off to 75mph for Sprinters and 60mph for other trains. At the *New Cut,* the river was straightened out when the line was built while within the cut-off loop the YNM built a standard terrace of three houses. These isolated platelayers' dwellings had no access other than along the railway, household coal being dropped off from the pickup goods. The houses have vanished but one ornamental tree from their gardens remains.

Huttons Ambo, looking towards Castle Howard. Note the typical NER slotted post signals and how the down home is located on the same side as the up home so it can be sighted round the sharp curve. Photo: J. F. Mallon.

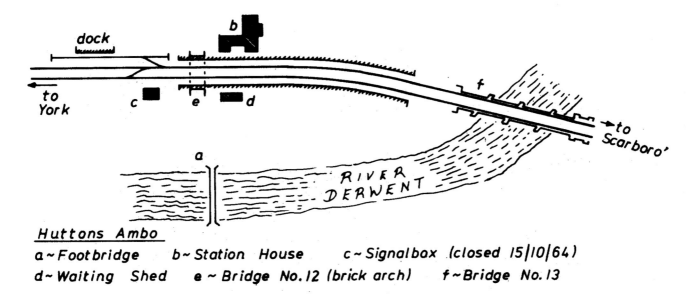

dock

to
York

a

RIVER
DERWENT

to
Scarboro'

Huttons Ambo

a ~ Footbridge   b ~ Station House   c ~ Signalbox (closed 15/10/64)

d ~ Waiting Shed   e ~ Bridge No.12 (brick arch)   f ~ Bridge No.13

Station Diagram: Huttons Ambo

4. Malton

Approaching Malton there used to be another sand siding coming in from the south. Sand and gravel workings were long established here and both the YNM and NER quarried gravel on Earl Fitzwilliam's land for track ballast.[11] Malton West Signalbox controlled access to the goods yard, engine shed and other sidings serving an iron foundry, manure works, timber yard and latterly the bacon factory. *Malton Farmers' Manure & Trading Company* was an important customer, despatching almost 5,000 tons of manure by rail in 1913.

The YNM's wooden roadbridge over the Derwent carried a siding to the imposing Derwent Mill, which is contemporary with the railway. Though the mill soon fell out of use, this line was revived in 1887 when the building became a biscuit factory. This venture also failed and the premises were then taken over by the Brandsby Agricultural Trading Association (BATA). Rebuilt by the NER in 1870, the bridge has wrought-iron girders and elegant cast-iron railings.

The gasworks was also on the opposite side of the river from the railway but much further upstream, beyond Malton Bridge. Coal had to be carted almost half a mile and there were negotiations about building a siding but the NER expected a contribution towards its cost, and in 1895, faced with a demand for £946, equivalent to the cartage bill for almost 40,000 tons, the Malton Gas Company decided it wasn't worth their while.[12]

For a time, Malton was the fifth busiest station on the North Eastern Railway for livestock traffic, handling 124,146 animals in 1914, and there were extensive loading docks.[13] These were conveniently close to the Derwent bridge but cattle had to be led right through the town centre to the Mart, and it is strange that the latter was never resited near the railway. Horseboxes were normally attached to passenger trains and so the original horse dock was at the east end of the down platform. Displaced by the Whitby Bay, the dock was resited on the south side of the line, a more convenient place for the racing stables, which are located towards the Wolds.

At its peak the railway provided over a hundred jobs in Malton and Norton, now down to just three. An omen was the failure to

A train from York heading into Malton during the nineteen-fifties, hauled by D49 Number 62702. In the background, two livestock vans stand on the track leading to the cattle dock. Lurking behind the signal and characteristic NER swan-necked water column is a very dirty G5 (NER Class O) Number 67315. Photo: J. W. Armstrong (photographer) J. F. Mallon collection.

Still-life in 1971. The throat of Malton goods yard, with a typical Bray-Waddington yard crane - though its wooden jib has been replaced by a steel one. Behind are the water tower and pumping house, water being drawn from the River Derwent. To their right stood the horse stable. Photo: Bill Fawcett.

118

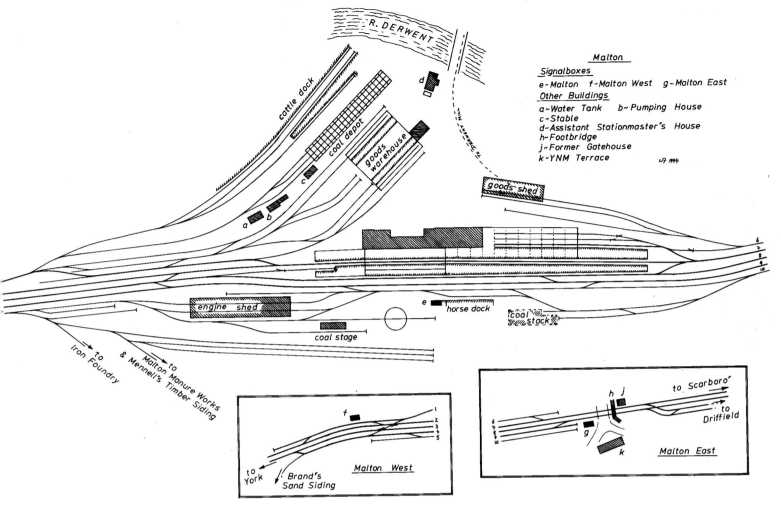

Station Diagram: Malton.

replace the goods station when it burned down in July 1956, while the engine shed closed in 1963, its last working being a return trip to Whitby on 13 April by an ex-LMS 2-6-0, Number 43055. The most dramatic blow was the closure of the Whitby Branch to passengers in 1965. It remained open for freight to Pickering (actually Hargreaves' quarry at New Bridge) until the following year, then Malton was no longer a junction and had no need of the elaborate railway infrastructure which had accompanied this role. Demolition of the shed took place in 1965-66 accompanied by a drastic simplification of Malton's track layout and extensive resignalling. Goods facilities were gradually run down, and finally abandoned on 3 September 1984 with the closure of Malton's public delivery siding. By 1995 there were just the two running lines and two rather neglected sidings, while the goods yard had been developed for housing.

Malton station is much reduced in scale, the up platform having been removed in 1966 and all traffic handled at the other instead.

A busy view of Malton goods yard showing the variety of traffic still carried on as late as 1961. Wagons stand on the coal depot in the centre, with perishables vans, tanks wagons and livestock vans to the left. On the right is the burned-out shell of the goods station. The only element of this scene to survive today is the agent's house, seen behind the coal depot. Photo: J.F. Mallon.

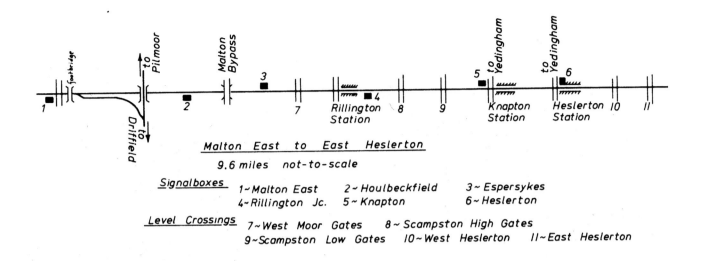

Line Diagram: Malton East-East Heslerton.

The building was listed by the Department of the Environment, chiefly on account of the historic value of its trainshed, so its subsequent history is somewhat ironic. Following storm damage, the glass was removed from the skylight of the trainshed and several years later British Rail received planning consent for its demolition. As a sop to conservation, part of the Whitby bay roofing, removed at the same time, was used to replace it but the job was only half done, leaving much of the rear wall of the station building standing bare. Today's streamlined railway only requires the waiting area and booking office, currently staffed for one shift on weekdays. The rest of the building is redundant but commercial development is expected to bring it into use and provide income, meanwhile, the site of the Whitby bay has already been developed for a supermarket. Across the road, Malton Bus Station, built by the West Yorkshire Road Car Company, is a reminder of the former integration of bus and rail services pioneered by the LNER.

5. Malton to East Heslerton Crossing

Leaving Malton, we pass the one remaining signalbox, controlling the crossing of the former A64, the scene of tremendous traffic congestion until the building of the Malton Bypass in 1978. Beyond this was the junction for the Driffield line, whose tracks ran alongside for a further quarter mile before heading south at the site of the original Norton Town Junction.[14] Then come the remnants of the girder bridges which bore the Thirsk & Malton line across the river and railway. No trace is evident of the wooden Norton Viaduct which originally carried the Scarborough line over the wetlands bordering the Derwent but something doubtless survives within the railway formation.

From here to Ganton the railway keeps to the southern fringe of the bottom of the Vale of Pickering. Straight and virtually level for most of the way, this is the fastest stretch on the route. Formerly it was subject to a line speed limit of 70mph but, with improved permanent way and the automation of many crossings, most of it can now be traversed by Sprinters at 90mph (70 for other trains), with some minor local restrictions to 80mph.

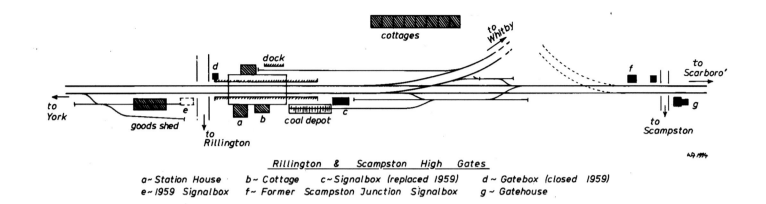

Rillington & Scampston High Gates

a~ Station House　　b~ Cottage　　c~ Signalbox (replaced 1959)　　d~ Gatebox (closed 1959)
e~ 1959 Signalbox　　f~ Former Scampston Junction Signalbox　　g~ Gatehouse

Station Diagram: Rillington and Scampston High Gates.

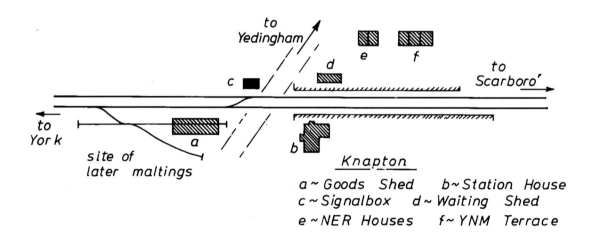

Knapton

a~ Goods Shed　　b~ Station House
c~ Signalbox　　d~ Waiting Shed
e~ NER Houses　　f~ YNM Terrace

Station Diagram: Knapton.

Rillington Junction in 1952 with a train taking the Whitby line in front of the 1873 signalbox. On the right is the short bay platform originally provided for Whitby trains. Photo: J. W. Armstrong.

High Scampston Gates about 1971. Note the NER revolving board crossing signal, a reminder of early-Victorian signalling practice, with which the gatekeeper warned trains that the crossing was in use. The relative peace of this area may vanish if the A64 is realigned to follow the railway in order to bypass the villages. Photo: Bill Fawcett.

When the block system was first introduced in 1873, the four-mile stretch between Malton and Rillington was split by an intermediate box at Houlbeckfield. To cope with summer traffic another was later provided at Espersykes, open only from July to September. The latter closed during the First World War, though it was not abolished until 1928. Under British Railways, Houlbeckfield was restricted to Summer opening and eventually closed. During the winter of 1993-4 a programme of level crossing automation brought the closure of many gateboxes and block posts, so today the first signalbox out of Malton is Weaverthorpe and the next is Seamer West.

As the original junction for Whitby, Rillington had a short bay at the east end of its down platform where Whitby trains stood before the connection was moved to Malton. For the first twenty years, passengers between Scarborough and Whitby had to change either at Rillington or Malton but on 1 July 1865 a through service was introduced and, to avoid trains reversing at Rillington, a curve was installed between Marishes Junction, on the Whitby branch, and Scampston Junction, on the Scarborough line. With a daily average of only 31 passengers, the service was withdrawn at the end of September 1866 although it surfaced again in the working timetable for August 1870.[15] After some years of disuse the track was taken up in 1880, and two years later the Forge Valley line opened, providing a direct route from Seamer to Pickering. Though the trackbed of the curve has now been ploughed, a lineside fence is still visible as is the route of the Whitby Branch itself.

Rillington signalbox was at the east end of the station, overlooking the junction, so that a small wooden gate box had to be provided for the level crossing at the opposite end. Both were replaced in 1959 by a new box at the crossing, now itself gone. Thus railway employment has ceased in this village as in most others. By comparison, in 1875 the long YNM terrace, still standing near the former junction, housed five platelayers, two signalmen and a porter.[16]

Continuing east we come to Scampston High Gates with a curious building on the left some distance before the crossing. This is the base of the former Scampston Junction signalbox, dating from 1865, adapted as a platelayers' hut and the oldest surviving signalling structure on the line.

At Knapton, the railway crosses the former York-Scarborough turnpike, heading towards Yedingham Bridge at the head of the extended Derwent Navigation. In North Eastern days there was a small yard with a G. T. Andrews' goods shed but, unusually, no coal cells, those at Rillington and Heslerton being considered quite near enough. During the nineteen-fifties large silos were built here to handle barley for malting; brought in from farms by road and then forwarded by rail. They still flourish but the rail connection has vanished.

Knapton's existence as a station probably stemmed from its location on the turnpike. East and West Knapton could barely be described as villages but it also served Scampston, accessible by a footpath across the fields, and Wintringham, three miles away in the edge of the Wolds. The station house is close to the Haxby design, though with a projecting porch (like Andrews' station at Shincliffe, near Durham, built a year earlier) instead of the doorcase. In 1908 an additional bedroom was built above the waiting room and the difference in brickwork is still clearly visible.

Heslerton Station was originally just a modest single-storey building. A curious feature was the signalbox, based on the NER's Southern Division design but oriented to have its gable end facing the tracks, a very unusual arrangement adopted also at the next station, Weaverthorpe. At one time, both signal boxes contained ticket racks in a section screened off at the rear.[17]

6. East Heslerton Crossing to Seamer

Sherburn Station, as it was originally known, served that substantial village about a mile away. The NER, having two other Sherburn stations, renamed it to avoid confusion. On 1 April 1874 it became Wykeham, named after a village three miles to the north but in 1882 Wykeham got its own station on the Forge Valley line so the North Eastern, in an inspired moment, renamed this one Weaverthorpe, after a village almost five miles away on the opposite side of Sherburn Wold. Like its name, the station house looks a little mixed up - essentially a Haxby design but with a rather incongruous hipped roof.

Knapton Station, looking west in April 1959. The YNM goods shed is dominated by the vast bulk of the then relatively new silos. Note the contrasting brickwork where the stationmaster acquired an extra bedroom. Photo: Ken Hoole.

Heslerton Station, seen soon after the house gained its upper floor in 1870. The first vehicle behind the engine, an unidentified 2-2-2, is a guard's van with its raised lookout. Photo: Ken Hoole collection.

Heslerton Station in 1959, looking west. Note the signalbox with its gable end to the tracks and the survival of the timber waiting shed almost thirty years after closure. Photo: Ken Hoole.

Weaverthorpe Station showing the signalbox, station house and signalmen's cottages. Photo: C.B. Foster.

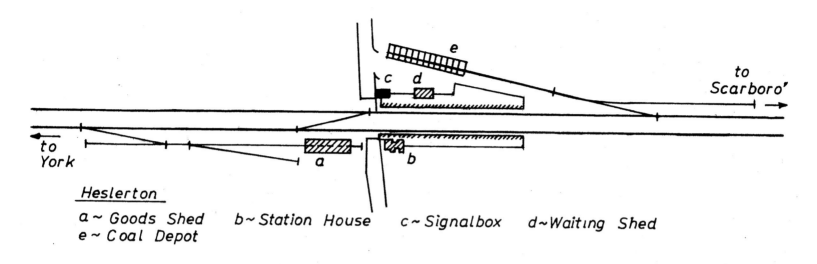

Station Diagram: Heslerton.

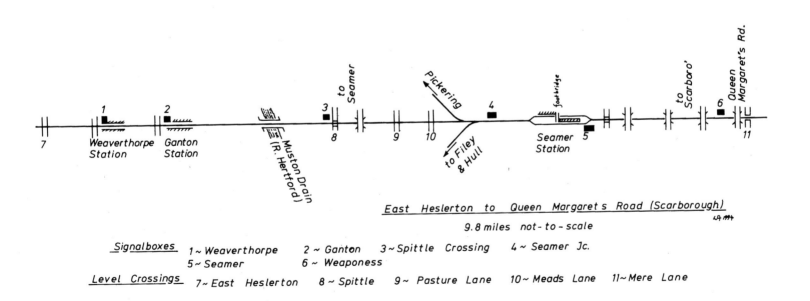

Line Diagram: East Heslerton-Queen Margaret's Road (Scarborough).

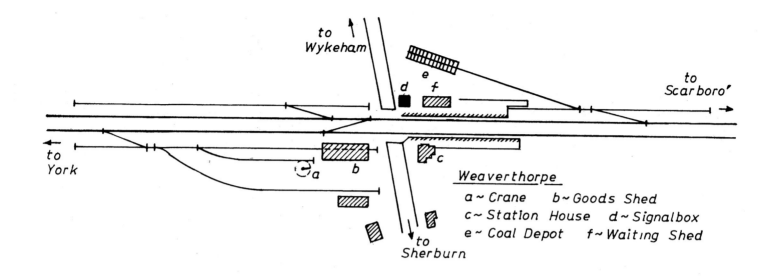

Station Diagram: Weaverthorpe.

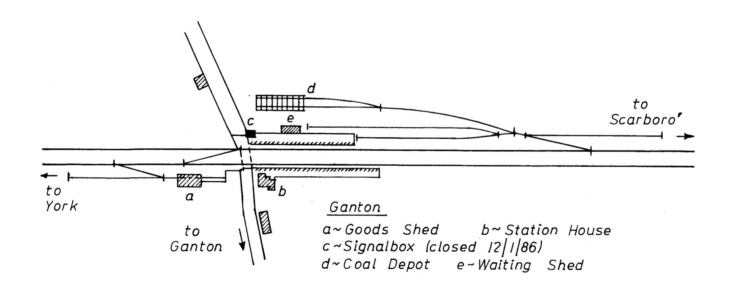

Station Diagram: Ganton.

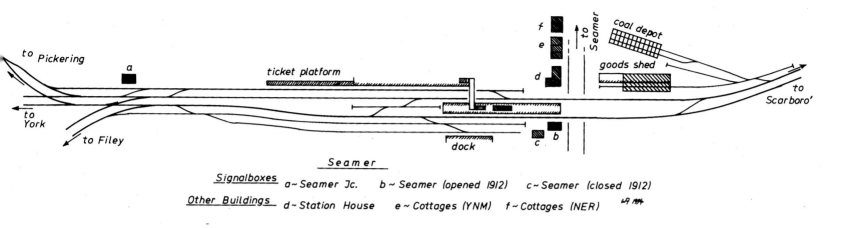

to Pickering

to York

to Filey

ticket platform

f

e

to Seamer

d

coal depot

goods shed

to Scarboro'

a

dock

c b

Station Diagram: Seamer.

__Signalboxes__ a ~ Seamer Jc.   b ~ Seamer (opened 1912)   c ~ Seamer (closed 1912)

__Other Buildings__ d ~ Station House   e ~ Cottages (YNM)   f ~ Cottages (NER)

Ganton is barely two miles from Sherburn, and its purpose was probably to provide a railhead on the roads to Beverley and Filey. In Edwardian times it became known for its Golf Club, founded in 1891, which provided a modest boost to NER income. Goods traffic was sufficiently extensive to warrant the NER providing a new goods shed which appears to date from the eighteen-seventies. The station house has been totally rebuilt.

Beyond Ganton the line curves northwards, heading over the flat lands of Willerby Carr and Seamer Ings, reclaimed bogland which may have caused construction problems like those recorded beyond Seamer. At Spittal there was a level crossing over the Scarborough-Staxton turnpike. This later became part of the A64 and a replacement bridge opened in 1936 under the same improvement programme as that at Barton Hill.

7. Seamer to Mere Lane Crossing/Queen Margaret's Road

Approaching Seamer, there were extensive sand and gravel workings, the latter once a source of track ballast. At Seamer Junction the coast line comes in on the right; on the left is the site of the Forge Valley route, closed in 1950 and demolished as far as Thornton Dale in 1952. The signalbox (now Seamer West) dates from 1906, when a down independent line was added between the junction and station, serving a ticket platform which replaced the Scarborough one displaced by Londesborough Road Station.

Seamer Station has an island platform, reflecting its former role as an interchange station between the York and Hull trains, although passengers are now encouraged to make the connection at Scarborough instead. Over a mile away from Seamer village, it is located between the considerably expanded villages of Crossgates and Eastfield.

Ganton Station, looking west, with the goods shed in the background. Photo: C. B. Foster collection.

The island platform at Seamer Station in 1978, with the goods shed being demolished in the background. This shows the picturesque collection of wooden waiting sheds which preceeded the present "bus shelter". Photo: Bill Fawcett.

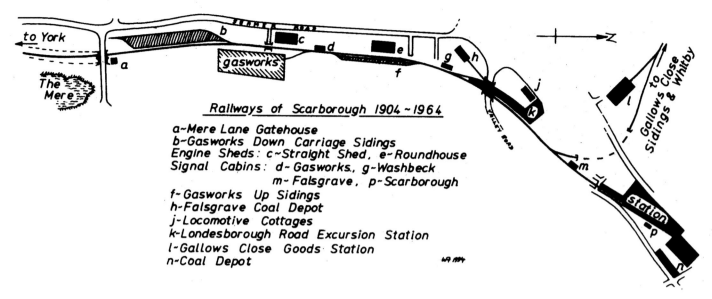

Railways of Scarborough 1904~1964

a~Mere Lane Gatehouse
b~Gasworks Down Carriage Sidings
Engine Sheds: c~Straight Shed, e~Roundhouse
Signal Cabins: d~Gasworks, g~Washbeck
                  m~Falsgrave, p~Scarborough
f~Gasworks Up Sidings
h~Falsgrave Coal Depot
j~Locomotive Cottages
k~Londesborough Road Excursion Station
l~Gallows Close Goods Station
n~Coal Depot

Railways of Scarborough 1904-1964.

In 1912 an additional down platform was brought into use, served by the down independent and reached from the island platform by a footbridge. A new Seamer Signalbox (now Seamer East) had already opened at the level crossing but its 1873 predecessor was not demolished until 1994. While the independent was of undoubted value as a place to queue trains at busy times, the platform fell into disuse and its typical North Eastern footbridge was dismantled in 1953 for re-use at Billingham.

Although the station house was a normal YNM design, the island platform had a curious waiting room, apparently contrived from two NER pent-roofed waiting sheds joined back-to-back and sheltering under a platform awning with columns of a distinctly second-hand appearance. Despite vigorous local protests, this curious but effective ensemble has been needlessly swept away and replaced by a standard glass shelter. Seamer was the last place to retain one of the original wooden goods sheds, demolished in 1978, and handled livestock traffic for the nearby Auction Mart. In later years all this business went by road, and now the mart itself has been replaced by a supermarket.

Given that three routes, two of them very busy holiday lines, converged at Seamer Junction, one of the mysteries of NER policy is why they failed to widen the line between there and Scarborough to four tracks. Having got powers to do so in their 1901 Act and purchased most of the land needed, they then sited the new Seamer signalbox in such a way as to obstruct the widening, which would have entailed a complete remodelling of the station and goods yard. Had the scheme gone ahead, the company would have been obliged to replace the level crossings by overbridges largely at their own expense. This may have been a discouragement but happened anyway, though driven by the need for road improvements so most of the costs were met from public funds.

Passing under the bridge which has replaced Seamer Crossing, we head towards the Weaponess Valley, encountering a further two bridges serving the Seamer Bypass, the second of which is a 1961 replacement for a NER bridge which had replaced the original Musham Gates crossing. The line then skirts the nose of Musham Bank to enter the valley, passing the site of Weaponness signalbox, a summer block post closed at the outbreak of the Second World War.

Continuing past the Mere, once bounded by the railway but now an ornamental lake screened from it by a tree-lined embankment,

Class 47 locomotive Number 47052 heading past Seamer's twin signalboxes on 28 May 1978 with a return excursion. Photo: C. B. Foster.

A view across Scarborough shed yard towards the South Cliff almost a century ago, giving some idea of the extent of the land taken up by the railway on its approach to theit own. McDonnell Class 59 0-6-0 Number 497, in original condition, takes water next to a line of twenty ton coal wagons. Behind can be seen the start of Gasworks Up Sidings. Photo: J.F. Mallon collection.

we reach the site of Mere Lane Crossing, closed but retaining its YNM gatekeeper's house. Under its 1901 Act the NER had proposed a bridge here, with Scarborough Corporation contributing £500. Fed up waiting, in 1927 the Corporation decided to build it themselves, estimating costs of £6,478 for the bridge and £10,514 for the roadway and approaches, to be partially funded by a loan from the Government's Road Board.[18] In November 1928 the LNER agreed to contribute 50% of the cost of the bridge alone up to a ceiling of £3000, estimating annual savings of £209 in crossing keeper's wages which should have been enough to finance this. The bridge is in two spans, leaving room for a pair of extra tracks on the up side. Mere Lane now bears the more imposing title of Queen Margaret's Road.

Beyond here the valley became industrialised with the resiting of Scarborough gasworks, and shows little hope of recovery despite the demise of this and the railway sidings and sheds which followed. On the left were Gasworks Down carriage sidings followed by the engine sheds described in Chapter 5. The 1890 straight shed eventually fell victim to subsidence and that half of it nearest the running lines was demolished, a makeshift wall of corrugated cladding being tacked onto the roof columns along the former centre line. Outside this, the uncovered tracks became a storeyard for mothballed locomotives in the last years of steam, which was also the final role of the roundhouse.

After the shed closed on 20 May 1963, the coaling stage was abandoned although some facilities were provided for visiting excursion locomotives until the end of steam in 1967. One fitter was retained to deal with minor faults on diesel and steam locomotives and railcars and, for a time, the clerk from the shed office operated from the stationmaster's office, dealing with the handful of drivers retained for railcar and shunting duties. The rump of the straight shed was speedily despatched but the roundhouse stood until June 1971. Now the only railway facilities on site are a turntable and water supply for visiting steam excursions. Gasworks Down Sidings have vanished, while Gasworks signalbox, latterly open during the summer months only, closed on 30 May 1965 and the impressive McKenzie & Holland signal gantries which once spanned the lines nearby vanished with it.

A brief break in the ribbon of former railway land is made by Seamer Street after which the former Falsgrave coalyard opens up on the left, retaining the YNM depot house at its entrance.

This was the site of the town's first oil depot, established by the Anglo-American Oil Company in 1896 and followed by Shell and BP. Latterly, oil traffic was handled at a depot established by Appleton Associates at the north end of the Gasworks Down Sidings site. With the disappearance of goods trains this had to be served by its own special trains, an uneconomic way of working requiring tank wagons to be detained there for long periods until the next train, and this traffic has now been lost.

On the left of the line was Washbeck signalbox, controlling access to the east end of the engine sheds and Londesborough Road Excursion Station. That station having closed, the track layout was simplified and resignalled so as to be controlled from Falsgrave box, with Washbeck closing on 17 May 1970. The station platform remains as do the original YNM enginemen's cottages.

A little further on we reach Falsgrave signalbox, always the most important of Scarborough's boxes and the only one left following the closure of the station box on 22 October 1984. On the left, behind the west end of the very long platform 1, is the walled up tunnel which brought the Whitby line in from Gallows Close. After bridge number 25, carrying Belgrave Terrace (formerly Love Lane), can be seen the world's longest platform seat extending up to the former excursion waiting rooms. Home for many years to the parcels office, and now housing engineering staff, they retain a section of the 1883 platform roofing, similar to that at Malton. Other than this, platforms 1 and 2 are now bare to the elements but this hardly matters since they are rarely used. Regular trains use platforms 3 and 4, with the York service concentrated on number 3. The station coal depot fell out of use in 1959 and was demolished two years later to make way for Tesseyman's Garage, now also gone and replaced by shops. Platforms 6 to 9 have also been removed but the buildings housing them, the former goods shed and link span, remain as a feature of a carpark.

Scarborough's 1890 straight shed with the mainstay of the coast route to Whitby, Class W. Designed by Wilson Worsdell as 4-6-0's but extended by Raven who converted them to Pacifics. Number 693 had been rebuilt in 1916. Photo: J. F. Mallon collection.

Scarborough's postwar B16 (NER Class S3) Number 61445 trundles the coal train from Gascoigne Wood past Washbeck Signalbox, with its conspicuous balcony. Behind the train can be seen two of the typical NER signal gantries together with the three gables of the 1881 roundhouse. Photo: Ken Hoole.

A Worsdell 4-4-0 heading a NER express from Leeds into Scarborough Station past the then quite new 1908 Falsgrave Signalbox. The signal gantry was replaced in 1934 during the construction of platform 1A.

Appendix 1: Operating Results for 1848

Table A1.1 Revenue & Expenditure on the Scarborough line and Pickering Branch

1. Revenue for these lines and the York-Normanton Main Line

Total goods and passenger revenue:	£230,571
Less passenger duty at estimated compound rate of 5% on passenger receipts of £108,033:	£5,402
Estimated Net Revenue	£225,169

2. Operating Costs of York-Scarborough and Pickering Lines

2.1 Locomotives and Train Crews

108,978 passenger train miles at 1.2p/mile	£1,308
85,222 goods and mineral train miles at 1.5p/mile	£1,283
	Total £2,591

2.2 Other Known Wages

51 men on permanent-way maintenance	£2,067
19 gatekeepers, signalmen and pointsmen	£681
40 men in coaching dept.	£1,934
23 men in goods and coal dept.	£1,096
	Total £5,778

NOTES

1. Unknown costs include maintenance of carriages, wagons and buildings (all new), permanent-way materials, rates and the appropriate share of the running costs of York's passenger and goods stations.

2. Revenue, train miles and other staff wages are derived from the *Third Report of the YNM Committee of Investigation*. The train miles are based on those for the first six months of 1849, simply doubled.

3. Locomotive costs are based on two main sources:
Train crews - typical wages of 30p/day for a driver and 20p/day for a fireman are quoted by Thomas Cabry in his evidence to the YNM Committee of Investigation, in *PRO Rail 770/12*. I have assumed one crew could complete two return passenger train journeys or one return goods between York and Scarborough in a day.

Locomotives - Coke consumption of 30lbs/mile for a new Stephenson long-boiler locomotive is taken from evidence to the Gauge Commissioners quoted in Ahrons: *The British Steam Railway Locomotive from 1825 to 1925* (pub. 1927), together with a figure of 0.4p/mile for repairs. A coke cost of 30p/ton is taken from NER statistics. Water and locomotive stores are estimated at 0.1p/mile, based on the ratio of these to fuel costs current on the NER in 1881.

Table A1.2 Revenue & Expenditure on the Whitby & Pickering Line

1. Revenue

Total Goods and Passenger Revenue	£11,194
Less passenger duty at 5% on passenger revenue of £4,545	£227
Estimated Net Revenue	£10,967

2. Operating Costs

2.1 Locomotives and Train Crew

65,244 mixed train miles at 1.5 p/mile	£979
40,274 goods & mineral train miles at 1.5p/mile	£604
Total	£1,583

2.2 Other Known Wages

27 men on permanent-way maintenance	£1,095
1 gateman, pointsman or signalman	£33
10 men in coaching dept.	£621
8 men in goods and coal dept.	£365
Total	£2,114

3. Financial Return

The balance remaining from the net revenue after deducting these costs is £7,270. This is equivalent to an Operating Ratio of 35%. Given the unknown cost factors, it does not seem particularly harsh to estimate the actual operating ratio at 40%, leaving a net return of £6,716. On a capital investment of £341,478, even before allowing for the renewal of permanent way, locomotives and rolling stock, the return is below 2% and explains the shareholders' dissatisfaction with their Whitby investment.

A notable feature of these statistics is the very low wage bill.

Appendix 2: Early Locomotive Workings at Scarborough

The following catalogue listing some of the locomotives working passenger services on the York-Scarborough line between 1880 and 1890 was compiled by Ken Hoole from the articles by E.L. Ahrons published in the Railway Magazine.

1. Engines based at Scarborough.

Fletcher Class 25 2-4-0's numbers 25, 26, 250 and 257, built at Gateshead Works in the eighteen-sixties.
Class 686 2-4-0's numbers 696 and 699, built in 1870.
Class 162 number 162, rebuilt from 2-2-2 to 2-4-0 in 1879.
Former Stockton & Darlington Railway 4-4-0 number 1165 was available as a spare engine.

2. Engines based at York.

Class 25 2-4-0's numbers 463 and 473.
Class 544 2-4-0's numbers 546, 551 and 552.
Class 686 2-4-0 number 698.
Class 1440 2-4-0 number 1441.
All these 2-4-0's were built between 1864 and 1876.
2-4-0 number 76 built 1853.
Class 220 2-2-2's numbers 66, 220, 224, 225 and 258.
Class 447 2-2-2's numbers 161, 280, 447-9, 450-2.
All these *singles* were built in the eighteen-fifties and sixties.

Appendix 3: Morning at Malton, 1898

Arrivals and departures of passenger and goods trains at Malton on a summer weekday morning up to 10 a.m. are taken from the 1898 NER Working Timetable.

arrive	depart	description
04.14	04.25	Coal train (limited stop): York-Scarborough
04.40	05.20	Cattle train: York-Scarborough, Tuesdays only.
04.57	05.02	Express passenger (mail train): York-Scarborough.
05.25	05.35	Goods train: York-Whitby.
—.—	06.00	Cattle and coal train: Malton-Driffield, Tuesdays only.
06.33	06.36	Slow passenger (mails for country stations): York-Scarborough
—.—	06.40	Passenger (& mails): Malton-Pilmoor
06.50	07.08	Goods train: York-Scarborough - *see Note 1*
07.25	07.28	Slow passenger: Scarborough-York
—.—	07.40	Passenger (& mails): Malton-Driffield
—.—	07.45	Passenger: Malton-Gilling
08.31	08.34	Express passenger: Scarborough-Leeds (arr. 9.50)
09.01	09.04	Express passenger: Scarborough-Leeds (arr. 10.25)
09.07	—.—	Passenger: Pilmoor-Malton
09.38	09.42	Express passenger: York-Scarborough
09.33	09.47	Slow passenger: York-Scarborough
09.40	—.—	Cattle and coal train: Driffield-Malton, Tuesdays only
09.53	—.—	Passenger: Driffield-Malton
About 10.00		Coal train (stopping): York-Scarborough
—.—	10.00	Goods and coal train: Malton-Driffield
09.50	10.05	Slow passenger: Scarborough-York
10.00	10.02	Express passenger: Scarborough-Leeds (arr. 11.10)

Note 1: on Mondays runs about 30 minutes earlier and picks up cattle at stations between Malton and Seamer for Seamer Auction Mart.

References

Abbreviations:

PRO ....Public Records Office, Kew
YCA........................York City Archives
YCL ....York Central Library
YG ....Yorkshire Gazette
SG ....Scarborough Gazette
SCL........................Scarborough Central Library
BoT ....Board of Trade
Tomlinson ..............W.W. Tomlinson: *The North Eastern Railway - Its Rise and Development*, published 1914.

CHAPTER 1

1. W.C. Copperthwaite: *Statistics of the Town and Parishes of Malton*, published in D.J. Salmon: *Malton in the Early Nineteenth Century*, North Yorkshire Record Office Publication No. 26, 1981. Copperthwaite's statistics, collected in 1841 and updated to 1844, are an invaluable record of the town just before the arrival of the railway.

2. K.A. MacMahon: *Roads and Turnpike Trusts in Eastern Yorkshire*, York & East Yorkshire Local History Society Publication No. 18, 1964.

3. White's Directories of *York & West Riding - 1838* and N*orth & East Ridings - 1840* (YCL).

4. Copperthwaite op. cit.

5. Although the GNE opened to coal traffic on 4 January 1841, the formation was not fit to carry passenger trains; these began on 30 March.

6. For the Rennie schemes see YCA DP2/10, 11 and 17.
For the first Stephenson scheme see YCA DP2/9
A guide to the deposited plans is provided by W. Fawcett: *A Descriptive Catalogue of the Deposited Railway Plans Held in York City Archives*, published by York University in 1994.

7. The final Stephenson scheme is YCA DP2/19. By 1844 Parliamentary standing orders required railway Acts to include a clause providing for public roads to be crossed by bridges. The Lords duly inserted such a clause (clause D) but followed it by another exempting the YNM from its provisions except in respect of Thief Lane, in York, and Washbeck Lane and Love Lane in Scarborough. Their select committee reported that *if bridges were required... over all or most of the roads the expense would be disproportioned* (sic) *to the remuneration expected, and amount to a prohibition of the undertaking*. Specific engineering objections to bridges, such as flood risk or excessive gradients on the altered roads, were tabulated by the committee in Appendix D to their report. (House of Lords Journal vol. 76 pp. 311-15)

8. YCA: York City Council 29 April 1844.

CHAPTER 2

1. YCA DP2/19 - Book of Reference. 466 letters of assent/dissent were sent to landowners along the route and produced only 46 objections; some would have been multiple responses from individuals in respect of different plots of land. (House of Lords Journal vol. 76 p. 313)

2. PRO Rail 770/2: YNM Board 3 July 1844.

3. The final land cost is given in the fourth report of the YNM Committee of Investigation, published 21 December 1849 (PRO Rail 770/13). Comparable figures for the original YNM and the GNE are given in Tomlinson pp. 355,6.

4. Crawshaw v YNM: Many construction details are taken from PRO Rail 770/26 - a volume of evidence in the arbitration between Crawshaw and the YNM held in December 1849. Of at least 3 books, only one survives.

5. The (now-buried) viaduct is shown with 12 arches on the 5 feet/mile York O.S. map published in 1852 (YCL) but is said to have 11 in a contemporary account of the opening.

6. PRO MT6 2/59: letter from Maj. Gen. C.W. Pasley of the BoT to the Earl of Dalhousie, 5 July 1845, re. the line's inspection.

7. Contemporary accounts of the opening are found in:
i) Eastern Counties Herald: 10 July 1845
ii) A reprint from YG in Burdekin's Old Moore's Almanac for 1917 (YCL).

8. Gateshead Observer: 2 August 1845.

9. PRO Rail 770/2: YNM Board 2 February 1846. Ballasting of the second track was still incomplete six months later: see Rail 770/3: YNM Board 20 August 1846. The second track was opened without BoT approval: see BoT letter of 8 August 1846 in Rail 770/34. During the bill's passage through Parliament, Scarborough Corporation had petitioned, requesting that it be rejected unless the YNM would undertake to lay a double track; their objection was on safety grounds and well-founded.

10. D. Beckett: *Stephensons' Britain*, David & Charles, Chapter 5.

11. YCA BC7/1: Ouse Navigation Committee Minute Book 1837-46.

12. PRO Rail 527/30: NER Locomotive Committee 13 December 1872.

13.A minor slip of the riverbank was reported in YG 2 April 1876. For developments see YCA Ouse Navigation Committee: 10 August, 13 September and 10 October 1878.

14. PRO Rail 770/3: YNM Board 18 June 1848. It was built to serve the Royal Agricultural Society's Show, which Hudson brought to York for the first time (see City Council minutes).

15. Crawshaw v YNM op. cit.

16. PRO Rail 770/3: YNM Board 30 July 1846 (also 18 September 1845).

17. YG 1 March 1867.

18. PRO Rail 390/62: LNER Traffic Committee min. 2289 of 29 June 1933 records this and the readiness of the North and East Riding county councils to take it over.

19. Malton Messenger December 1869 recorded the start of rebuilding.

20. YG 14 March 1868.

21. PRO Rail 527/35: NER Locomotive Committee: min. 21270, 10 March 1881.

22. PRO Rail 527/27: NER Locomotive Committee: mins. 7137 (21 October 1864) and 7344 (5 February 1865).

23. YG 17 October 1868.

CHAPTER 3

1. The Builder, 17 August 1844.

2. PRO Rail 770/2: YNM Board 6 February 1845.

3. G.T. Andrews' original drawing for Scarborough Station is held in the Victoria & Albert Museum Print Collection. Other sources for the early railway layout in SCL are an Admiralty Survey of Scarborough, published October 1847, and the O.S. 5 feet/mile map, published August 1852.

4. PRO Rail 770/12: YNM Committee of Investigation - evidence of G.T. Andrews, 27 July 1849.

5. John Bearup, Scarborough's stationmaster from 1870, retired in April 1882 to take over the hotel and refreshment rooms. The hotel was probably given up when the NER took over management at the start of 1897 - see PRO Rail 527/94: NER Hotels Committee, 30 April 1896 and 30 March 1897.

6. A drawing of Malton Station, showing the original appearance of the trainshed, was held in the British Rail (now Railtrack) York Plan Room - ref. microfilm reel 97, frames 52-4.

7. For Flaxton see PRO Rail 527/68: NER Traffic Committee 4 November 1880.

8. PRO Rail 527/644 Contracts Summary Book p. 62 records that work started on 28 March 1887, finished on 1 November and cost £1,910.

9. PRO MT6 15/46: Report of BoT Inspection on 6 October 1857.

10. PRO Rail 527/1303: NER Architect's Contract Summary Book.

11. PRO Rail 527/1145: NER 1862 Survey of Cottages. A further schedule was made in 1875: Rail 527/952. Neither includes station houses.

12. The third anniversary of introducing the block is reported in YG 8 July 1876.

13. PRO Rail 527/644

14. Engine shed does not appear on first edition O.S.

CHAPTER 4

1. Copperthwaite op. cit. Stephenson's estimates for passenger traffic (including road carriages, horses and mails) were revised down to £14,421 when the bill came to Parliament. (House of Lords Journal vol. 76 p. 313)

2. From fourth report of YNM Committee of Investigation, 21 December 1849.

3. Tomlinson p. 356. The 1844 Act permitted the YNM to raise £86,200 in loans as well as the £260,000 capital.

4. Same source as 2.

5. PRO Rail 770/12: YNM Committee of Investigation - evidence of John Cass Birkenshaw, 16 August 1849.

6. C. Hadfield: *Canals of Yorkshire and North-East England*, pp 440-4.

7. Richardson & Gutch, in private practice in York, were solicitors to the NER. A resume of the transfer to the NER appears in PRO Rail 390/63: LNER Traffic Committee min. 2510 of 26 July 1934, just before the LNER handed the Derwent Navigation over to the River Ouse Catchment Board.

8. Birkenshaw's report is in YCA: York Local Board of Health 9 November 1852.

9. For mail arbitration see PRO Rail 770/3: YNM Board 27 April 1848 and 23 November 1849.

10. PRO Rail 527/62: NER Traffic Committee min. 3497 of 11 September 1857.

11. Wages quoted by Thomas Cabry in his evidence to the YNM Committee of Investigation on 27 July 1849. (PRO Rail 770/12).

12. K.O.M. Golisti: *The Gas Adventure & Industry at Malton*, Malton, 1985.

13. NER Mineral Statistics, published 1915, author's collection.

14. PRO Rail 770/14: Cabry's reports to YNM Board, see report of 17 September 1851 announcing the opening of the new depot on the following Monday.

15. Fish Traffic from PRO Rail 527/2074: NER Accountant's monthly returns.

CHAPTER 5.

1. A thorough account of this line is given in P. Howat: *Railways of Ryedale and the Vale of Mowbray*, Hendon Publishing Co., 1988.

2. PRO Rail 527/23: Joint Locomotive & Stores Committee of the YNM, YNB and Leeds & Thirsk Railways (working arrangement prior to forming NER) - 8 July and 5 August 1853, and 3 March 1854.

3. See PRO Rail 527/63: NER Traffic Committee mins. 4739 and 4809 of 1861; Rail 527/26: NER Locomotive Committee 22 November 1861 and 29 August 1862.

4. The NER advertised for tenders for a new shed in June 1866 but opted for extension instead, advertising in YG 2 March 1867.

5. PRO Rail 527/62: NER Traffic Committee min. 3142 of 21 November 1856, but no follow up in this committee.

6. PRO Rail 527/24: NER Locomotive Committee min. 2420 of 30 January 1857; 3174, 3206 and 3259 of 1858; 3816, 3955, 3998 and 4269 of 1859.

7. PRO Rail 527/526: plans of three alternative schemes for resiting Scarborough Goods Station, no date but before 1878.

8. PRO MT6 209/5: Major Marindin's BoT inspection report of 21 June 1878, with a NER plan of the new station layout.

9. The progress of these works is chronicled in PRO Rail 527/644, a NER Architect's Office contract summary book which gives details of contractors, costs and start and finish dates. See page 39 for this roof over the *express platforms*.

10. PRO Rail 527/644 page 50. The excursion station works cost £14,668.

11. These works began in September 1883, once the holiday season was over, and completion was signalled by the installation of the clock, illuminated by gas and supplied by Potts & Son of Leeds, at the end of June 1884. The total cost was £6,575.

12. The decision to move the gasworks is reported in SG 30 January 1873 and the new works is described in SG 6 April 1876.

13. The locomotive yard connection was inspected by Maj. Gen. Hutchinson of the BoT in October 1880 (PRO MT6 261/11). Completion of the shed is documented in PRO Rail 527/644; it cost £4,376.

14. The stable provided 21 stalls and 3 looseboxes but had to be supplemented by stabling for a further 6 horses in 1898 and 9 in 1901.

15. See plan in PRO Rail 527/562.

16. PRO MT6 326/20: Major Marindin's BoT report of 11 January 1883.

17. PRO MT6 843/4: Col. Addison's BoT report of 10 August 1898.

18. The goods station cost £8,715.

19. NER land in Scarborough is shown on two maps in PRO Rail 527/772.

20. Work on the station began in August 1907 and the final building cost (i.e. excluding signalling and permanent way) was £7,634. The existence of two stations sometimes confused the unwary passenger, who arrived at Central only to find that their train was leaving from Londesborough Road. Suggestions for a footbridge to link their platforms came to nothing. Latterly an attempt was made to use Londesborough Road chiefly for charter excursions, whose stewards would be better able to ensure that travellers did not go astray.

CHAPTER 6

1. Train service developments are charted largely through Bradshaw and NER public timetables held in the National Railway Museum.

2. W.J. Scott: *North Eastern Coaching Stock* in Railway Magazine vol. V, 1899, p. 79. One beneficiary was George Gibb who, as NER general manager, lived in Scarborough and commuted to York. He also boosted traffic by founding York Golf Club, with a course at Strensall.

3. These runs were published in Allen's regular series on *British Locomotive Practice & Performance* in the Railway Magazine, and then reprinted by O.S. Nock in his book on North Eastern Railway locomotives.

4. Railway Magazine vol. XVII, 1905, p. 22 reports the NER autocar experiment.

5. See *NER Scarborough Passenger Station Summer Staff Arrangements for 1890*, operating dept. booklet in Ken Hoole collection.

6. From *NER Excursions & Special Trains from 25 August 1883*, operating dept. booklet in NRM collection.

7. Railway Magazine vol. IX, 1901, pp. 11,12,20. The London service started on 13 July, leaving Marylebone at 8.15 a.m. and reaching Scarborough at 2.45 p.m.

8. From NER operating dept. 1874 excursion programme booklet. NRM collection.

9. A handbook for this excursion, detailing trains, is in SCL.

10. Figures from PRO Rail 527/2074: NER Accountant's monthly traffic statistics.

11. Scarborough goods statistics from the goods agent's annual returns in J.F. Mallon collection. They differ slightly from the adjusted summaries kept by the NER accountant.

12. R.J. Irving: *The North Eastern Railway Company 1870-1914, an economic history*, Leicester University Press, 1976. The coal price rise was, fortunately, a short-term fluctuation.

13. The dispute is chronicled in SG from June 1873 onwards, particularly 17 July and 4 and 11 September.

14. NER Summer 1899 Passenger Timetable. NRM collection.

15. For more details see K. Hoole: *NER Buses, Lorries and Autocars*, pub. Nidd Valley Narrow Gauge Railways, 1969.

CHAPTER 7

1. The comparative mileages are pasted into the NER General Manager's Office copy of the NER 1922 summer timetable held in the NRM.

2. PRO Rail 390/61: LNER Traffic Committee min. 1621.

3. Based on annual summaries in PRO Rail 527/2142: traffic statistics for NER Southern Division stations up to 1926, with additional entries for 1934 and 1935.

4. PRO Rail 390/63: LNER Traffic Committee min. 2854 of 26 March 1936.

5. Annual report for 1934 by stationmaster F. Dowson to District Supt., York. Ken Hoole collection.

6. Report on 1924 summer working at Scarborough from A. Deighton, District Inspector, to District Supt. Ken Hoole collection.

7. Scarborough station operating schedule for August Bank Holiday 1956. K.C. Appleby collection.

8. F. Dowson op. cit.

9. Plan in J.F. Addyman collection.

10. Details in PRO Rail 390/61: LNER Traffic Committee mins. 1793,4 of 19 March 1931.

11. PRO Rail 390/41,2: LNER Property Committee mins. 2439 (1933), 2528 (1934), 2798 (1935), 3368 (1936).

12. PRO Rail 390/62: LNER Traffic Committee min. 1950 of 26 November 1931. LNER circular of 12 August 1931 detailing use of these vehicles, in Ken Hoole collection.

13. PRO Rail 390/63: LNER Traffic Committee min. 2639 of 28 March 1935.

14. PRO Rail 390/64: LNER Traffic Committee min. 2918 of 25 June 1936.

15. First report of LNER Postwar Development Committee, September 1943. J.P. McCrickard collection.

16. LNER Magazine, August 1946, p. 174.

CHAPTER 8

1. Trains Illustrated, January 1959, p. 34: *Diesel Traction in the North Eastern Region* reports a paper given by the region's Assistant Operating Officer, F.L. Hick.

2. Railway Magazine, March 1961, p. 155: *Trans-Pennine Diesel Trains*. G. Freeman Allen: *The Planning and Execution of the new Leeds-Manchester Service* in Trains Illustrated, April 1961, p. 200.

3. *The Reshaping of British Railways*, HMSO 1963, p. 14.

4. Stationmaster's annual return of traffic and staff for Malton in 1908. J.F. Mallon collection. The total excludes part-time staff and working pensioners.

5. PRO Rail 527/1695: Petition from shopkeepers of Norton re. expected job losses following retirement of John Baines from Southern Division Engineer's Dept. A letter from NER secretary, C.N. Wilkinson, on 9 January 1891 said only 8 jobs would be transferred.

CHAPTER 9

1. The principal sources for this chapter are Ken Hoole's draft manuscripts and notes on locomotives allocated to Scarborough shed, held in the Ken Hoole collection, together with the Railway Correspondence & Travel Society series of books on the *Locomotives of the LNER*, to which he contributed extensively. Other details are taken from the train register books of Ganton (J.R. Lidster collection) and Scarborough Gasworks signalbox (J.F. Mallon collection).

2. Railway Magazine vol. LXI, 1927, p. 489.

3. Railway Gazette 5 November 1943 contains a formal accident inquiry report. Scarborough Mercury 13 August 1943.

CHAPTER 10

1. PRO Rail 527/1145

2. YG 12 December 1879.

3. PRO Rail 390/61: LNER Traffic Committee min. 1701, 23 October 1930.

4. *The Reshaping of British Railways*, HMSO 1963, pp 99-101.

5. YG 24 February 1912

6. Strensall brickworks connection reported in PRO MT6 1026/3, BoT inspection by Col. van Donop on 8 August 1901.

7. The concessionary stop at Flaxton is listed in PRO Rail 527/1867, a 1905

survey of such arrangements.

8. PRO Rail 390/42: LNER Property Committee min. 3262 of 28 May 1936.
    PRO Rail 390/64: LNER Traffic Committee min. 2892 of 28 May 1936.

9. For description of this stretch of line and an account of Queen Victoria's visit
    see Ibbotson: *The visitor's guide to Castle Howard, 1851*. (YCL)

10. For the Burythorpe Light Railway see YG 26 July and 2 August 1913.

11. PRO Rail 527/26: NER Locomotive Committee for 24 October 1862 has
    Cabry reporting plans to open up a new ballast pit at Malton, replacing an
    existing one.

12. Golisti op.cit.

13. LNER (NE Area) Station Traffic Index, 1925, author's collection. Malton
    station annual returns for 1914, J.F. Mallon collection.

14. These tracks were probably added during 1880-82, see PRO Rail 527/36:
    NER Locomotive Committee 5 October 1882, and 527/34: NER Locomotive
    Committee decision of 6 November 1879 to alter the junction.

15. PRO Rail 527/34: NER Locomotive Committee on 20 November 1879
    decided to take up this curve and re-use the materials in forming the new
    connection to the Malton & Driffield line.

16. PRO Rail 527/952.

17. ex info. R.D. Pulleyn.

18. PRO Rail 390/60: LNER Traffic Committee min. 1241 of 29 November
    1928.

Index